PLANTS with STYLE

KELLY NORRIS

PLANTS with STYLE

A PLANTSMAN'S CHOICES FOR A VIBRANT, 21ST-CENTURY GARDEN

TIMBER PRESS • PORTLAND, OREGON

All photographs are by the author, with the following exceptions:
Phlox 'Forever Pink' (page 122) by Jim Ault; *Plantago major*
'Purple Perversion' (page 234) by Joseph Tychonievich.
Lettering by Michelle Leigh

Published in 2015 by Timber Press, Inc.
The Haseltine Building
133 S.W. Second Avenue, Suite 450
Portland, Oregon 97204-3527
timberpress.com

Printed in China
Cover and text design by Michelle Leigh

Library of Congress Cataloging-in-Publication Data
Norris, Kelly D., author.
  Plants with style: a plantsman's choices for a vibrant,
    21st-century garden/Kelly Norris.—First edition.
    pages cm
  Includes index.
  ISBN 978-1-60469-401-7
1. Plants, Ornamental. 2. Gardening. I. Title.
SB404.9.N67 2015
635.9—dc23   2015019577

CONTENTS

INTRODUCTION

A MANIFESTO FOR MODERN GARDENING

Landscaping is not a complex and difficult art to be practiced only by high priests. It is logical, down-to-earth, and aimed at making your plot of ground produce exactly what you want and need from it.

—Thomas Church, *Gardens Are for People* (1955)

This book takes a sassy, punchy, irreverent look at fresh plant choices for modern gardens, with sidelong glances, along the way, at how gardening is more relevant than ever to our quality of life. If gardening is about the experience, it stands to reason we should all be planting things worth experiencing. Such plants make a garden our own, and this book is about plants with style, those plants that matter. Its pages are for people who crave beauty and plant-filled spaces. Of all the gardens I've had the pleasure of visiting, the best prevailed because of what grew: plants, after all, are (or should be) the very essence of a garden's style.

Modern eclecticism is the 21st-century way—with access to almost anything, we have transcended the strictures of period and form. Our sense of style is expressed by the things we love, no matter their vintage or source. Unsurprisingly then, this book is a smattered collection, viewed through a garden's architecture, with chapters considering environment, structure, emblems, vignettes, and essential kitsch as lenses on an endless array of options—too many plants, too little time. Through this globetrotting, zone-straddling look at plants with style, I hope one thing becomes clear—a passion for vibrant, A-list plants is inextricably linked to my hope for a more beautiful, functional planet.

The modern eclectic garden isn't easily defined. It's earnest, enthusiastic, and unbounded. It grows from a kind of purposeful materialism—plants matter because they tell stories, reminding us of the journey and the experience of acquiring and assembling them into a space, a garden, that brings us joy. And this garden doesn't stand still. It evolves almost every day, tumbling forward headlong—just as its leaves, flowers, stems, and fruits do—because of its plants, its ingredients. Making the 21st-century garden requires not only carefully considered ingredients but smart recipes, too. Each of the five chapters—recipes, if you will—clarifies the modern garden's components, focusing on a chic shortlist of essential plants. So begins our journey, borrowing influence and inspiration from wherever it flowers.

It's one of the elegant simplicities of modern gardening—nobody has time to fuss over things that won't grow, that fail to do what they were planted to do. Plants in your garden should thrive, not just simply survive. For too long, horticulture existed in spite of our environment, instead of honoring and respecting it. Minding ecology and reveling in regionality make for environmentally successful gardens, sustained by thoughtful choices and made beautiful with artful planting. From coast to coast and borough to borough, the wild spaces of our world, sometimes not so far from home, offer incredible inspiration. After all, horticulture in tune with our environment is more than just a talking point that "sounds" good—plants chosen with that idea in mind will do better, naturally.

The Victorian Border, a seasonal display at Allen Centennial Gardens on the campus of University of Wisconsin-Madison. Former director Ed Lyon nevertheless embodies with this vignette the very spirit of the 21st-century garden: it is alive with vibrant color, contrast, and motion.

Gardening with purpose is the mantra of the modern era. People garden for more than just aesthetics or sustenance. People garden with intention, a grounding force in an otherwise chaotic world, where responsibility to community and planet is at least understood. We live in times when the quick tempo of life has become something to brag about, when even our vacations are chipped away at by links to the work we left behind. We seem to find less time to savor the things we love. A garden is the best way to savor life on earth. Purposeful planting begins with investing in a garden's structure, the long-tail pleasures of a garden's evolution. Structure in the garden isn't permanent, but it is defining.

We plant what we love, from rooted trees that make for vital shade to moving parts that remind us of the rhythm of the seasons—emblems. The resulting garden is a blend of things planted as solutions and others planted with revelry, a fondness for our relationship with change. Some plants solve the challenges inherent in making beautiful gardens. Others define the spirit of the garden through an untethered passion for the beauty of the planet. Gardens should be lived in and edited often. Weeding out, pruning, and composting previous decisions polishes and refines the garden. Call it compulsive, call it obsessive, or just dub it geeky and get on with it, gardening makes for a truly rich life.

We live in a beautiful world; gardeners should know the power of planting. Great gardens deserve great plants—a choir of the most talented singers. The garden's chorus is dynamic, full of vignettes that inspire us with a beauty that is in sync with the seasons. Follow your style or taste, whatever it is, and plant a garden that is distinctly your own. Don't wait to be inspired—find inspiration in everything. Furthermore, just as you don't have to be a fashionista to appreciate good clothing, you don't have to have botanical bona fides to grow great plants.

Geekiness has attained a sort of sex appeal in modern culture, from retro glasses and funky socks to the idolization of awkward mannerisms, rhetoric, and personalities in pop culture. Plant geeks are no exception, even if as we obsess over stamens and other minutiae, we may inadvertently intimidate the less impassioned among us. Cultivate your inner plant geek—it's sexy. The world needs more gardens, more beautiful spaces to unwind in and harvest from. Plant geeks cultivate the leading edge of the revolution—sometimes brandishing things deemed too kitschy for general consumption. I believe that many gardeners are in fact geeky plant collectors; they just don't know it or accept it. Don't sneak—show it off.

Finally, even as I attempt to remain practical in my treatments of the plants I celebrate in its pages, this book doesn't attempt to divulge every detail of their cultivation; rather, it is a rhapsody, a paean for a new romanticism born from passionate interaction with plants. In short, hunt up all the facts, if you want, before you commit shovel to earth, but in the end, grow plants, garden with them. To know them is to study them, and experience is the best teacher. For those so smitten, garden because you have to and hope others join you along the way.

This book is a story of my own passion for searching out, trialing, and promoting hardworking, thriving plants for cosmopolitan landscapes—plants that gardeners haven't seen and that ultimately deserve wider recognition. There are surely more omissions than inclusions. What gardener, really, isn't in pursuit of plants? I garden because I want a world full of damn cool plants, teeming with spirit and style. I see that as the ideal for so many gardeners, whether they're twenty-five or seventy-five. So why have we settled for typical gardens filled with boring, lackluster plants that don't excite or enliven? Why have we become a culture of shy, reluctant gardeners? I have a feeling that many of us want something different, and we rightly should demand it from the people we buy plants from and the people we look up to for gardening ideas. Call it a revolution or a quest for gardens that make sense, this book is a call out for a new generation of passionate, motivated, and enthusiastic gardeners who love to play in the dirt.

ENVIRONMENT

PLANTING AT THE INTERSECTION
OF PLACE AND ECOLOGY

Until recently the standard approach to the home landscape included a large expanse of grass lawn, disciplined beds of annuals, and brutally pruned shrubs. In most cases, the wisdom of such a landscape went unquestioned, even though homeowners were actually battling nature instead of working with it.

—Ken Druse, *The Natural Garden* (1989)

Gardening in harmony with the environment is the new vernacular. Recognizing that gardens aren't isolated from the world around them and leveraging that to your advantage is sure to result in a more satisfactory gardening experience—plain and simple. Giving a damn about our environment, about how it looks *and* how it grows, is the conscientious thing to do, a spirit that should be planted deeply into the beds and borders that extend our homes. Stylish gardening is about connecting with the earth. The best gardens are created when we embrace sense of place and celebrate ecology.

The first element of making beautiful gardens, then, is not so much the stylistic persona you'll employ in its later development but the context in which it exists—its foundation, in other words, to settle on just one of the many apropos analogies. I sometimes think of gardens as houses, built so many stories high (or not), with walls and floors to spec, rooms or nooks at every turn. Like a house, a garden is to be decorated and lived in. Gardeners, by extension, are artists at work—dreaming, scheming, crafting, and planting their way to some kind of ever-evolving, playful finale, which, unlike the house itself, is never really all that final.

In a garden that borders parkland in Savannah, Georgia, borrowing the nearby live oak laden with Spanish moss (*Tillandsia usneoides*) might translate into finding a tree to dress with this common bromeliad, the obvious promulgation of sense of place.

(left) In the beginning, making a garden is about the plants that form the foundation of what you're about to build—the plants that connect a garden to your environment, whatever it may be.

In the Desert Southwest, regionally centric planting invokes the shape and colors of fishhook barrel cactus (*Ferocactus wislizeni*), repeating spiny themes abundant in the desert backdrop.

(left) On the prairies, wind-blown grasses carry on phantom waves the mantra of modern ecology with each midsummer gust. These matrices of deep-rooted perennials teach us to think about communities of plants, thriving together in a delicate but plantable balance.

In urban environments, look to what colonizes buildings, bridges, and overpasses. Plants like Boston ivy (*Parthenocissus tricuspidata*) or English ivy (*Hedera helix*) have no place in smaller, intimate landscapes, where their brutish personalities might overwhelm everything. But forced to scale the monuments of modern civilization, they work hard to soften lines and edges.

EMBRACE:
Planting with What Grows Around You

Finding inspiration in the context of where you garden is critical, because it's what personalizes the garden. Plants may drive the design, but sense of place gives a garden its soul. Gardens in hardscrabble neighborhoods are grounded by incorporating rough-hewn features, repurposing found objects, and letting plants fill the voids between the hardness of humanity. Those built atop a breezy hillside have see-through plants that frame views and tolerate wind. A wet spot in the backyard or the burning hellstrip next to the street prompts, at either extreme, garden making of an entirely pragmatic though no less stylish kind. The inspiration for building a new garden can quite often come from something much bigger than the property itself. Hilltop or not, it's called borrowing the view, taking note of what extends beyond the garden's edge and putting it to work. Sometimes it's about repeating what's germane to the rest of the landscape; at other times it's about juxtaposing it. Partnering with nature, whether original or contrived, is essential for creating a sustainable space.

Certain plants dutifully evoke a sense of place, some greater feeling about the landscape that littler pieces can't quite express. They consort with their surroundings as a result of evolution and environmental

Texas firecracker bush
(*Anisacanthus quadrifidus*).

adaptation. In the context of their space, they are the right plants for that place. It follows that in every climate, some plants' personalities (and so often their nativity) beg to be amplified.

While place may define your environment, your sense of style colors within the lines. And while your environment may well define your palette, it never has to limit it. Gardens should be outgrowths of their surroundings, even if as expressions of their creators they seek to convey something unfamiliar. You won't be the first to create an Asian garden in the middle of the desert, for example. In hot, exposed, waterwise gardens, the fiercest colors deserve serene coordinates. The wailing red flowers of Texas firecracker bush (*Anisacanthus quadrifidus*) or California fuchsia (*Zauschneria californica*) cry for cool companions: try Mexican blue sage (*Salvia chamaedryoides*) or Santa Barbara sage (*S. leucantha* 'Santa Barbara'). Add the blades of *Agave desmettiana* 'Joe Hoak' or *A. havardiana* to at once unify the vignette and tie it to the greater landscape, with pointed rosettes of accenting and contrasting colors.

Almost every garden I've ever explored in the Pacific Northwest causes me to consider scale. There, the boreal native landscape celebrates evergreens like western red cedar (*Thuja plicata*) and Douglas fir (*Pseudotsuga menziesii*). Often shrouded in foggy cloaks, the permanent, static scaffolding of these trees frames the landscape in distinctly regional terms, while the cultivated landscape revels in Asian natives

(clockwise from top)
Agave desmettiana 'Joe Hoak'.

Mexican blue sage
(*Salvia chamaedryoides*).

Agave havardiana.

A slough of ferns (including *Adiantum* and *Polystichum*) and Spanish bluebells (*Hyacinthoides hispanica*) looks authentically Left Coast, reveling in seasonally abundant moisture as observed here at Hatley Park, Royal Roads University, Victoria, B.C.

that are at home in the Left Coast's similarly maritime climate. Notable and obvious among these are the Japanese maples (*Acer palmatum*).

Underneath the Pacific Northwest's well-architected canopies flourishes a palette of plants adapted to shade, acidic soils, soggy springs, and rainy autumns with a three-month dry spell in between. Ferns like *Adiantum aleuticum* and perennials like *Trollius laxus* symbolize the natural "gardens" that populate the wild slopes of the region's mountains and forests. But in a climate so generous and paradisial (did I mention mild winters?), it is tempting to garden with plants from anywhere. The Chinese native *Beesia deltophylla*, the rare and unusual groundcovering relative of buttercups, is one such example, forming glossy carpets that rival freshly varnished floors for sheen and shine. Tough, sturdy foliage seems to soak up the downpours of spring just enough to last through the lingering dryness of summer. Outside the Northwest, it grows with mixed success. It wilted into a disheveled salad in my loamy Iowa garden a few summers ago, but I've admired fine masses of it in Michigan in the same months. In flower it's airy and elegant, with foamy white stars that alight on delicate, ascendant stems.

On a plant hunting trip to the Black Hills one July, I found myself at sundown immersed in a shortgrass meadow that embodies perfection in my memory unlike few other vistas I can recall. Silver, shield-sized leaves of the deeply taprooted balsamroot (*Balsamorhiza sagittata*) and

Beesia deltophylla.

(right) If you've never dreamed of a meadow front yard, start now. Imagine the possibilities.

ascendant spears of white sage (*Artemisia ludoviciana*) knit themselves together in a tight weave, growing in communal competition. Two plants made this vignette magical, a simplistic matchup of dynamic foliar personalities and a reminder that less is so often more. In an area of the country so sparsely populated, taking in this view seemed like a rare privilege. In the same meadow on the other side of the hill, the pattern repeated itself, only with additional elements. Absent the dramatic leaves of the balsamroot, the texture was finer, instead drawing on the subtler contrasts in color between the silver leaves of the artemisia and the bubblegum and blue flowers of *Astragalus laxmannii,* a legume known only to rock gardeners unfortunately, all arrayed amid a bladed carpet of sedges, sand lovegrass (*Eragrostis trichodes*), and prairie junegrass (*Koeleria macrantha*).

(clockwise from top)
A prairie dominated by indiangrass (*Sorghastrum nutans*) near my hometown in southwest Iowa stands as a reminder of the frontiers of biodiversity that remain unexplored by most gardeners. They thrive by the thousands, locked in an ecological dance with goldenrods (*Solidago*) and big bluestem (*Andropogon gerardii*).

Little bluestem (*Schizachyrium scoparium*).

Japanese apricot (*Prunus mume*).

In the Midwest, grasses like indiangrass (*Sorghastrum nutans*) and little bluestem (*Schizachyrium scoparium*) bring motion to the garden, catching the spirit of the prairie from the winds that rustle through their culms. Growing up and traipsing through the remnants of formerly expansive prairies, I relished these grasses as they tickled my legs and arms. Both indiangrass and big bluestem (*Andropogon gerardii*), the taller cousin of little bluestem, are remarkably absent from North American gardens, even though at one point in biogeographic history they were nearly the most populous plants on the continent. New cultivars of indiangrass from Iowa State University offer a glimmer of hope for the species as it slowly earns some street cred as a garden staple. 'Bantam', a dwarf, and 'Redspike', an aptly named variety with red-tinted spikes, join 'Indian Steel' and 'Sioux Blue' as some of the only representatives of this species on the marketplace. The latter two, besides evoking nonexistent rock bands in name, really earn points for their pewter and aquamarine leaf blades, respectively.

Venture to the Deep South and you'll undoubtedly encounter southern magnolias (*Magnolia grandiflora*) and Japanese apricots (*Prunus mume*). The southern magnolia is instantly "known" to us, familiar from historic paintings, novels, and movies that depict the story of the American South. With hefty, glossy leaves and a broad canopy, a singular Southern magnolia speaks southern in a dialect that few plants can. Japanese apricots, the favored geishas of the southern winter garden, are thirty years into their life in American horticulture, elevated from obscurity by famed plantsman J. C. Raulston in the 1980s. In the eyes of plantsmen, it's the belle of cold months, coveted for its pink and white rosettes that dangle charmingly in a lonely season, when little else matters. I'm giddy at the mention of it, recalling the first time I encountered the plant in Tennessee in mid-February—the perfect grace note for a winter blues day. While the flower colors are relatively limited—white and red forms mark the ends of the spectrum, with most coming in near pink—the international sentiment they express is more than enough to make up for it. Hovering over the doorstep, framing the entrance to the house, a Japanese apricot now couldn't look more quintessentially southern.

In the Northeast and Great Lakes, I love encountering sugar maples and the various fiddlehead ferns (*Osmunda cinnamomea, Matteuccia struthiopteris*) in well-mannered abundance, icons of the eastern North American forest. This native landscape is an ecotone that expands over millions of acres and a dozen states. As home to our country's earliest settlers, this portion of the continent arguably shows the greatest impact of humanity on the native landscape. At the margins of development, natives and nonnatives mingle precariously in ecological imbalance. Yet further into the wild, beyond the greater metropolises of the coast, tall groves of hardwoods still shade lush carpets of ferns, ephemeral wildflowers, and shrubs that were the beginning of America's horticultural heritage.

Spicebush (*Lindera benzoin*), an eastern native to be prized, earns few raves nowadays, despite its near essential role in delivering the earliest doses of color in spring. Tiny yellow flowers dot the gray stems of this large upright shrub that Thomas Jefferson valued for its potential use as a flavoring. In fall, the plant reprises its role in the garden as an effusive source of beaming yellow.

Sweet fern (*Comptonia peregrina*) and Rhode Island have a lot in common, primarily that neither of them is what their name describes. A singular relic of a genus long extinct, this stemmy shrub grows three to four feet tall often in the companionship of pines on sandy soils, though it adapts to a range of loamier soils, particularly in garden settings. Texture is the operative word, as its common name suggests—ferny, frond-like leaves extend in waves from leathery stems that age to bronze in the waning days of autumn.

The fact is that within any one region, there are dozens of plants that characteristically define the garden. Regardless of style, incorporating at least some of these in the garden's palette bodes well for some semblance of ecological authenticity. The native plant movement has long called on a gardener's civic duty by appealing to environmental responsibility. That message has given way to a lasting, sustainable paradigm of American horticulture. When we plant natives, we embrace our environment. Embracing what we have, for its opportunities and challenges, means at the core we are taking inspiration from the environment at large and accepting responsibility for it. That's not to say just because you support local farmers that you can't have a good Bordeaux on occasion. Similarly, just because you embrace your local plant palette, doesn't mean you can't celebrate wild gems collected from around the world. The lines of ecology and evolution aren't as easily drawn as the boundaries of continents or geopolitics. As a design idea, it makes sense to embrace sense of place. As a model for ecological goodness—the harmony of living in context—it's more than sensical; it's golden.

(clockwise from top)

Spicebush (*Lindera benzoin*).

Sweet fern (*Comptonia peregrina*).

An expansive colony of ostrich fern
(*Matteuccia struthiopteris*) at Coastal Maine
Botanical Gardens, Boothbay, Maine.

CREATE:
Making The Garden with What You Have

With a solid ethos rooted in embracing our environment, we can more confidently approach the challenges of making gardens while simultaneously reveling in the rewards. Celebrating plants, after all, gives gardening its thrill; the merrymaking is in the details—but that comes later. Connecting a garden to environment starts not only by considering how the space is to function but by frankly acknowledging soil, light, and the domination of climate and its range of temperatures. To prioritize the discussion, I've charged off hardiness and functionality to peripheral conversations. The functionality of any garden space is a subjective choice, one the gardener must make when charting a new horticultural adventure. Hardiness is all encompassing—plants either are hardy in your garden or they are not. Thus, the two biggest considerations when starting a new garden, renovating an old one, or retouching an existing one are soil and light. Remember, no matter your circumstances, there are almost 250,000 known species of flowering plants: there *is* a plant that will thrive, whatever challenges a garden presents.

YOUR SOIL ISN'T AS BAD AS YOU THINK

No matter what you call it—soil, dirt, mud—the rawest of the elements you'll face when making a garden is the stuff underfoot. Gardening on less than desirable soil seems to be the norm—at least you'd gather as much over weekly coffee with your gardening friends. In short, everyone thinks their soil sucks. Mention clay to a fellow gardener and you'll likely get a grimace in return. While some gardeners in the western United States might bemoan their sand and constant aridity, surely the fiercest enemy in the fight for good gardens everywhere is clay soils, those that have a higher ratio of clay to silt, sand, or organic matter. Gardening in clay soils isn't exactly the kind of bliss most gardeners look forward to as they leave the house, tools in hand on a summer morning. Too often, gardeners struggle with clay, feeling the urge to do battle against the soil instead of accepting the nature of the dirty world below their feet; but as they quickly learn, clay soils tend to become elastic, spongy, and slimy with the addition of water and, in drier periods, firm, rigid, and sometimes powdery to the touch.

Regardless of how bad you think your soil is, gardening on it isn't impossible, even if at first it seems more like battle and war than love and peace. To borrow a saying—garden smarter, not harder. Let's raise a trowel to working with the soil you have. There's a cast of plants ably suited to the challenge.

The André Bluemel Meadow at the American Horticultural Society's River Farm represents the ultimate alternative to the traditional American lawn with four acres of woven grasses and forbs nestled along the Potomac River.

MARVY MILKWEEDS

Unfortunately the reputation of milkweeds stretches unfairly between two poles—on one end sits the smashingly orange but sort of commonplace butterfly milkweed (*Asclepias tuberosa*) and on the other the weedy and dastardly common milkweed (*A. syriaca*). Don't get me wrong, I secretly like them both (the former far more than the latter) for their intense durability under a variety of conditions. Even if the usual butterfly milkweed packs an ordinary punch, the color variants are where the KO is. Various shades of red and yellow grow on the benches of nurseries, often propagated from local populations and sold under various names. The reds have a rusty quality to them; the yellows verge on golden. My favorite is a dwarf yellow form (sold under that description) I picked up at The Flower Factory near Madison, Wisconsin. It flowers profusely on stems half as tall as the usual variety.

Lovely as they are, this sampling of the milkweed tribe is remarkably shallow. With a genus numbering some 140 species (over seventy of which are native to North America), the possibilities for finding the right plant for the right place are far greater than what available offerings would suggest. At the top of my list, at least in terms of their garden worthiness, are two co-reigning champs. Though not a plant for the stickiest of clay, purple milkweed (*Asclepias purpurascens*) grows across a remarkable range in the wild, inhabiting dry, rocky glades and moist, shaded, lowland savannas, where it often grows contentedly in some clay. In the Ozarks, it's an effortless addition to the understory. In the garden, it's a plant that requires some patience, like all comely milkweeds. But while you're being patient those first few years or so, the roots of your purple milkweed mine themselves deep into the ground, establishing a dense taproot with a network of woody roots—all words you want to read in the description of a clay-busting plant. When finally established, the rewards—vibrant, rouge-colored flowers—are worth the wait. Equally slow but just as valuable is the redring milkweed (*A. variegata*), a native of the eastern United States that bears delicate clusters of pearl flowers with a distinctive red halo. Rarely encountered, its presence in a garden means two things—someone has impeccable taste in milkweeds and a security system armed to ward off would-be looters. In short, a plant worth cosseting, once you lay hands on a division.

(clockwise from top left)

Butterfly milkweed (*Asclepias tuberosa*).

Purple milkweed (*Asclepias purpurascens*).

Redring milkweed (*Asclepias variegata*).

BLUESTARS

Bluestars (*Amsonia*) are close kin of milkweeds, recently classified as belonging to the same family (Apocynaceae). For those less concerned with taxonomy, the lessons of the family are worth repeating—bluestars, like milkweeds, have a predilection for growing in tough soils, from clay to sand. In the wild, these sixteen or so North American natives grow from the Desert Southwest in loose scree to the East Coast in woodsy humus. In the garden, they are bellwethers of spring's climax. Four earn appraisals here. The first, *A. tabernaemontana* 'Short Stack', is a dwarf form of the common eastern bluestar, a distinctive specimen with little penchant for reseeding. As much as I love the bluestars, they can be a weedy bunch, shooting umpteen little bluestars into the garden universe, often where you least want them (the only wish you'll make on these stars is that they shed a thousand instead of ten thousand seeds). Tony Avent's 'Short Stack' short circuits those genetics, at least in my experience, politely filling out its border home with nothing but charm and grace. A little taller is *A. illustris*, an inland relative of *A. tabernaemontana* found in the south-central Plains and the Ozarks. With glossier, narrower foliage and pendent seed pods, its ornamental effect is subtle by comparison but still desirable.

In stark comparison to those already mentioned, the ciliate bluestars (*Amsonia hubrichtii* and *A. ciliata*) sport filigree foliage that turns

Threadleaf bluestar (*Amsonia hubrichtii*) in glorious fall color.

enviable shades of gold and yellow in autumn. If you haven't heard, there's nothing unexpected about the color of bluestar flowers—they are blue, on a scale of silvery to periwinkle and only rarely white. Their value lies in their flowering time and plant habit. If you're looking for an unusual form of these fringy bluestars, seek out *A. ciliata* 'Georgia Pancake', flat from the frying pan of this meritorious plant. "Had I the heavens' embroidered cloths," they'd hardly compare to the golden rug of this plant in fall color. Did I mention that all these are deer resistant? Their virtues are endless.

NOTHING FALSE ABOUT FALSE INDIGOS

Growing up, I poked around prairie remnants in southern Iowa, seeking out plants that fascinated me with their beauty in otherwise bygone places. Welcoming them to my garden didn't seem novel or part of a movement—it was an answer to a child's fascination with flowers so close to home and yet so precious and rare. Among these plants, which I admittedly failed to cultivate with success until I was older, were two false indigos—*Baptisia alba* and *B. bracteata*. The former is the prairie's version of a string of pearls, dangling along the upper lengths of four- to seven-foot-tall stems. Sculptural to an artist's eye, it's rare in gardens, probably because it doesn't fit the paradigm of modern nursery production. Native plant nurseries occasionally offer it, though establishing it is a lesson in patience with a dose of memory loss and apparent neglect. To grow its umbrella of pressed, pea-like foliage and watch its flower buds spurt into these lithe and lilting stems is a precious blessing. Similarly, cream wild indigo (*B. bracteata*) remains one of the coolest plants on the planet, if I was inebriated enough to chart the list. It grows and flowers much closer to the ground than its tall, white cousin, a softer-shaded blossom skimmed from the finest milk. Tony Avent named a selection with generous clusters of ground-hugging flowers 'Butterball'. If I counted the number of times I'd failed at growing this plant, I'd run out of fingers. When I finally succeeded—the pitiful excuse for soil that it made roots in notwithstanding—all trials were forgotten.

Any one of the numerous new hybrids of false indigo makes a striking focal point in the spring garden. A three- or four-year-old established clump is enough to stop traffic, a natural response (sheer disbelief) to its busty presence in the perennial border. With showy hybrids like *Baptisia ×variicolor* 'Twilite' (Twilite Prairieblues) and *B.* 'Solar Flare' (Solar Flare Prairieblues), you can't help but want to dot a few of these in the roughest soil you have in an act of warfare-like defiance. False indigos have notoriously deep and fleshy root systems, ably suiting them to the stickiest of clay soils but also making them fairly recalcitrant to division at any time of the year except early spring. Small machinery, teams of sherpas, and archaeological permits may be necessary should you desire to relocate a toddler-aged specimen. The bottom line: site carefully and permanently. In turn, false indigos will reward the garden scene with hundreds of pea-shaped flowers spring after spring for much longer than you can imagine, much less intend. Who doesn't love a tough plant with values like commitment? Other new varieties worth naming include the Decadence series from Proven Winners, with diet-crashing names like 'Lemon Meringue', 'Cherries Jubilee', and 'Dutch Chocolate'. In short, most new varieties, regardless of their origin, reward similarly—bountiful floral displays, stocky architecture, and prairie-style star power.

Baptisia ×variicolor 'Twilite' (Twilite Prairieblues).

A seed-grown selection of *Oenothera macrocarpa* ssp. *fremontii* growing in my scree garden with flowers aplenty.

THE DAWN OF EVENING PRIMROSES

You'll surely pick up on a theme in this book before long—I feel a duty to champion genera that are either underrated or disregarded entirely. While I don't suggest the latter is true of *Oenothera*, it's certainly true that this amazing genus of so-called evening primroses, suncups, and sundrops hasn't gotten its due in the American garden. As if those common names weren't suggestive enough, the overwhelming majority of species and cultivars tend toward yellow and nearby hues. *Oenothera tetragona*, with its sun-soaked, bowl-shaped flowers, epitomizes the effect, and several of its cultivars have merit, perhaps because they thrive in everything from good, compost-heavy garden soil to the thin remnants of topsoil left in the hellstrip. 'Fireworks' is one of the best, with red buds giving way to a sunrise surprise (I'm always apt to give a plant points for a well-placed surprise). It's a consistent performer, never lacking for flowers even through the hottest days of summer. If you're with me in the surprise camp, you have to grow *O. versicolor* 'Sunset Boulevard' for its arresting crimson, amber, auburn, and maroon-blended flowers that make even the best tequila sunrise look like Kool-Aid. Backlight it and you'll faint.

If drunken celestial colors aren't your thing, you might consider *Oenothera macrocarpa* ssp. *fremontii*, which has the added benefit of scintillatingly silver foliage. Native to chalky, rocky soils (read: hell) in northern Kansas and south-central Nebraska, these silver salvers serve up yellow flowers, sunny and tastefully lemony, on the eve of high summer—an eloquent way of saying that these flowers show up when it's blisteringly hot out. Several nice forms and selections of this showy Great Plains native are available, with image-conjuring names like

Cercis canadensis 'Forest Pansy' seen from below, a scintillating reminder of the power of backlighting.

'Shimmer', 'Silver Wings', and 'Comanche Campfire'. Of these, 'Shimmer' has the highest "hot or not" score for its dazzling foliar presentation and floriferousness.

SHADY BUT NOT SKETCHY

Light is equal to soil in terms of its primacy in the garden and yet is the most under-realized character as a source of inspiration there. Consider this—light plays an enormous role in framing the views of plants in combination. Backlit, some take on a completely different personality; gleaming and glinting surreally, they look nothing like their appearance at high noon.

Then of course comes the practical application of light. Some plants need to grow in full sun, others in full shade. Some have evolved to make do in the middle, preferring a Goldilocks-blend of light and darkness throughout the diurnal cycle. In urban gardens, shade predominates due to the psychological yearning city dwellers and policymakers have for canopy, green space, and respite from the rigors of metropolitan life. In suburban and country gardens, wider vistas open up. By itself, the exposure of a garden poses few limitations to the plant palette, contrary to the long-held notion that shade gardens are the scourge of horticultural ambition. In fact, shade gardens don't have to become hosta ghettos underneath tall, old trees. Shady exposures offer as many possibilities for assembling a dynamic garden as sunny exposures, even if the characters that populate the scene prefer the darker corners of the garden.

×*Heucherella* 'Solar Eclipse'.

(left) A mosaic of silver and speckled leaves, heucheras and tiarellas carpet the ground of the trial garden at Terra Nova Nurseries, Canby, Oregon.

(top) 'Blondie' from Terra Nova's Little Cutie series is a smashing variety for the patio or windowsill, a houseplant heuchera that looks like something Penny Singleton might have cooked up if ever there was one.

Tiarella cordifolia 'Susquehanna'.

HEUCHERAS, HEUCHERELLAS, AND TIARELLAS

It's worth stating the obvious. What is there to say about coral bells that hasn't been said already? They are fabulous, leafy-luscious companions for just about any other perennial that hangs out in shady places—the cheese to pair with the wine. Without question, Dan Heims of Terra Nova Nurseries is the *Heuchera* dude, and his introductions best the too-many-to-count and too-many-to-grow varieties on the market.

Picking a few to highlight seems almost futile, but a handful of recent introductions deserve extra fanfare. The Little Cutie series stands apart from the rest for the diminutive size of its members. Perfect for containers, small dishes, and even windowsill gardens, these tykes flower profusely against a backdrop of foliage ranging from warm and copper to shiny and silver. My favorite of the bunch is 'Blondie', if only for the bakeshop contrast between its flowers and leaves—like frosting on a cakey square.

Foamy bells (×*Heucherella*) are the horticultural love children of coral bells (*Heuchera*) and foamflowers (*Tiarella*), and a fine expression of both parents at that. Many recent introductions seem to capture the roving nature of *T. cordifolia*, which I find desirable; some gardeners accuse this southeastern native of being rampant, but there are worse weeds to do battle against. Of the roamers, 'Yellowstone Falls' and 'Redstone Falls' from Terra Nova earn high marks for their spilling habit in containers or carpeting quality in the ground. 'Solar Eclipse' couldn't have a more descriptive name, even if my mind wanders, once again, back to the bakeshop when viewing its Hershey's-dark lacquered leaves edged in crisp mint. It's a clumper too, minding its crowns without wandering stolons to contend with, and when planted alongside something that converses with its mint edge, the effect is—in a word— jaw-dropping.

Finally, foamflowers. Tiarellas have unrivaled elegance when it comes to plants that form lovely carpets. I've been most impressed by the River series from Sinclair Adams of Dunvegan Nursery (the godfather of the heuchera-tiarella clan), which harken back to their native roots in style. 'Susquehanna' is my favorite, the shortest of the series and with the most heavily marked leaves. Nobody can argue with its rampant growth, which makes it a great groundcovering alternative to the boring something-or-others you've had to choose from. The series earns its keep in dry shade, in particular, where members seem to be right at home despite their water-inspired names.

Shredded umbrella plant
(*Syneilesis aconitifolia*).

(opposite) Mayapple
(*Podophyllum peltatum*).

THE UMBRELLA RULE?

A couple feet above the ground a few members of the shady characters gang occupy a uniquely low canopy. These umbrellas of sorts hover more than cover, and planting them for said effect utilizes them brilliantly. If you're looking for a savvy move to play on your gardening friends, consider planting either mayapples (*Podophyllum*) or *Syneilesis aconitifolia*. In different seasons, in different ways, these two very different plants accomplish the same thing—they disrupt the expectation that texture in the shade garden exists completely at your feet.

The North American mayapple (*Podophyllum peltatum*) looks great when viewed from above and excellent when viewed from below. How a gardener accomplishes this is entirely dependent on circumstance. I've always imagined planting them along a wall or a hillside where the grade drops off to permit viewing from beneath. However you can magnify the leaves of this plant, do it. In woodsy soils with ample moisture, you'll cultivate a colony of mayapples, which earn their name from the apple-esque fruits that follow delicate, white blossoms. From China, the related *P. hexandrum* and *P. pleiandrum* ratchet up the umbrella effect with considerable panache—bigger leaves, bigger clumps, and red fruits. Hubba, hubba, hey. All around, these deer-resistant plants will grow as much as your soil feeds them—more compost equates to more growth.

Particularly when accented from below by solid textures, the tattered leaves of shredded umbrella plant (*Syneilesis aconitifolia*) are nothing short of exquisite. A cold hardy perennial native to the Korean peninsula, this is one rhizomatous colonizer that no serious shade gardener should be without. In early spring, much like the mayapples, the whorls of palm-like, down-covered leaves pop from the ground like cocktail umbrellas at a luau. As they stretch higher, the leaves unfurl into beautifully dissected arrays. Most people pity the flowers, and while they are certainly not worth a stir, their wiry stems piercing the foliar canopy adds just another element of intrigue to a plant that already doesn't lack for it.

FLOWERS IN SHADE

Unlike the ragtag band of criminals masquerading as musicians in the 1955 black comedy *The Ladykillers*, the lady's slippers (*Cypripedium*) shout (quietly) class, even if they prefer the shadier corners of the garden. In spring, they reign supreme, holding forth in clumps of voluptuous flowers. Several species are worth extolling; all should clamor for your attention, but most are unfortunately quite expensive, mainly because it can take years to produce salable plants. New breeding work from Werner Frosch in Germany has produced several enticing interspecific hybrids, among them 'Gisela', 'Gabriella', and 'Anna'. The number of individuals advancing this genus seems to be increasing—if only the world had more lady's slippers, world peace might be within reach.

When obtainable, many of the native species settle in nicely given acidic soil and ample moisture. But make no mistake, these are not plants for the beginning gardener—for the price tag associated with the investment, it's wiser to take a chance only when you're sure you can give these collectables the conditions they need. Among the easier species to grow and obtain from nurseries are *Cypripedium reginae, C. kentuckiense,* and *C. parviflorum.* In woodland gardens with humus-rich soil, these pocketbook-shaped flowers borne on eighteen- to twenty-four-inch-tall stems will reward abundantly for years, the ultimate union of sexy and sustainable.

If I challenged you to make a list of plants that bloomed in electric colors in the shade from the high summer months through fall, you probably wouldn't end up with much of a list. My leading example is

Hoary skullcap (*Scutellaria incana*).

(right) Japanese woodland sage (*Salvia koyamae*).

hoary skullcap (*Scutellaria incana*), which grows in far fewer gardens than it should. First, it gets points for dry shade, owing that adaptability to its native home in the Ozarks. Second, its cobalt blue flowers arrive in July and August, just as the hostas start to give in to midsummer heat. It has a lax, though not floppy, habit and surely looks good mingling with *Hydrangea* or *Calycanthus* at the edge of the shade garden. Each little helmet-shaped flower gives way to cute, jewel box–shaped seed pods that contain one or two seeds. I've only experienced polite reseeding, but planted en masse, you're guaranteed a swoon-inducing show.

While most gardeners probably consider *Salvia* for the sunniest of exposures, a small band of Japanese natives prefers the cooler realms of the shade garden, cooler soils included. The first I gardened with was Japanese woodland sage (*S. koyamae*), a fabulous yellow, autumn-flowering herb that quickly fills out into a three-foot-wide and -tall mass of buttery awesomeness. Then I invited the hairless Japanese woodland sage (*S. glabrescens*) into my gardening life. Indignant at my ignorance of this species' existence, I was flattered by the cultivars 'Shi Ho' and 'Momobana', purple and hot pink, respectively. In the garden, they behave similarly to *S. koyamae*, preferring woodsy soils under a mostly shaded exposure. They too are fall-flowering, indeed among the last perennials to begin flowering in zones 5 and 6.

STRUCTURE

LIVING FRAMEWORK

Better off, I think, is the gardener who learns right off that a garden with permanent framework, no matter the size, is one that brings satisfaction to the four seasons while developing, along with its gardener, a sublime patina with age.

—Dan Hinkley, *The Explorer's Garden* (2009)

After settling on some environmental ethos of your own, building the garden, whatever its scale, starts with a solid framework. The modern garden deserves a durable skeleton: strong, living structure, walls and floors on which to hang and paint. For gardeners far more engaged by the details, structural plants can easily go unnoticed or overlooked, but they are essential for framing or blocking views and shifting perceptions. And just as in nature, structural plants have a way of uniting the landscape; they are leaders on a botanical scale. Their value in making gardens, however, is more than just the addition of woody and leafy architecture in positive space. Structural plants come to define spaces around them—the negative space—in ways beyond aesthetics. Practically, structural plants can shade the garden, filtering or blocking light entirely, or even pose an ecological threat to their planting companions—think about the effects of black walnut trees on the soil, as a common example. Yet, there is more to structure than simply what remains of woody plants long into the dormant winter. Consider the garden's permanent surfaces, chiefly the ground. What tree or shrub, aside from some aberrant prostrate form, can honor these surfaces? In all, structural plants begin to evoke the spirit of a garden, setting in motion the means to celebrate plants for their seasonal virtues and eclectic personalities.

TREES

Structural plants in the modern garden don't have to tower over everything. Not all cities have skyscrapers, after all. Few modern gardens have room to spare, and if they do, they are quite likely populated with large trees to begin with. Regardless of stature, structural plants should follow an ornamental orbit, a seasonal, months-long path through aesthetic virtues (not merely a one-off floral event) that warrant their planting. They should always have some trait that strengthens the garden's bones. In a garden that celebrates seasonality, you should plant to maximize every ornamental trait possible—berries to bark.

Structure then couldn't be more important—it provides the lines between which plant-driven ideas flourish. The lines matter, impermanent though they are. Like the average kindergartner on a quest to use every color in the crayon box, I once felt restricted by the lines and lacked the precision to color between them. As a style-conscious gardener, though, I've learned that a great garden arises from the sweet spot between constraint and creativity—unleash too much creativity and the garden becomes a smattering of discordant paint chips; constrain yourself too much and you'll end up with a space that's cold, lifeless, and unfeeling. Style is eternal—it's a lasting sense of who you are, even if your taste in plants changes over time. It's a look, once personalized, that nobody else can touch. It's yours, which means that if you can remodel the house, you can remodel the garden. A fifth of good bourbon before the chainsaw can certainly ease your discomfort (seriously, though: don't drink and operate a chainsaw!). A garden is a forgiving subject to changing expressions.

The gray birch allée, a "structure" created by preeminent landscape designer Warren H. Manning, draws people irresistibly into the surrounding landscape at Stan Hywet Hall and Gardens, Akron, Ohio.

TRUNKS

Let's start with a classic—redbuds (*Cercis*). Redbuds are some of the
most recognizable small flowering trees. With ten species native
throughout the world, these familiar legumes known for their lithe
stems in adolescence and knobby, contorted trunks in adulthood have
recently done an about-face, adding foliar excitement to an already staple floral display. These innovations signal plants of merit, the cumula-
tive efforts of independent plant breeders ignited by the same viral idea.

A species worth name-dropping up front is *Cercis racemosa*, a Chinese native appraised by the cognoscenti as having the finest flowers of
the genus—rich, dripping racemes of shell pink. Its hardiness is ques-
tionable though mostly untested. Gardeners in zone 7 and above should
have no trouble, but below that proceed with caution (or experimen-
tally). When successfully grown, this upright, vase-shaped tree frames
any walkway, gateway, or corner to perfection.

The newest hybrids have no lingering cloud of uncertainty over them.
Ray and Cindy Jackson of Belvidere, Tennessee, have released a series
of head-turning, press-warranting redbuds that could well turn a page
for the tree from timeless to trendsetting. The Rising Sun redbud (*Cercis canadensis* 'JN2') leads the pack with peachy new growth that ages
to golden tangerine and eventually lime green. The trees have a natural
weeping habit, for which I weep with joy. When I finally had a chance to

A decades-old eastern redbud (*Cercis canadensis*) extends its craggy trunks over the garden floor at Olbrich Botanical Gardens, Madison, Wisconsin.

Cercis canadensis 'JN2' (The Rising Sun).

(right) *Cercis* 'Whitewater'.

witness the cultivar in production on sandy bottomland fields in middle Tennessee, I thought I'd discovered the Holy Grail.

Denny Werner at North Carolina State University has taken the color-popping-leaves-plus-weeping-form equation and applied it in a cross of 'Covey' (marketed under the more descriptive name Lavender Twist) by 'Forest Pansy', the rouge-leaved redbud that I love to plant as a natural lamp shade. The result is 'Ruby Falls', a prolifically flowering, richly veneered tree that maintains its color throughout the growing season. For the drama geeks gardening after work, this tree is for you. Werner also hit a winner with 'Whitewater', a variegated weeping red-bud in the same foliar tradition as 'Alley Cat' (discovered by Allen Bush in, you guessed it, an alley) and 'Floating Clouds' (introduced by Don Shadow). Picture green leaves, flecked with white paint or just think Jackson Pollock in two colors. If you're into variegation, you'll need one or three.

Blackgums (*Nyssa*) come to mind when I think of lines and structure. Call it a bias, but I'm smitten. With such crisp, defined architectural branching in leafless seasons, the blackgums are the garden's scaffolds. Upright and pyramidal forms of the species are classic additions to the garden, whether in wet or normal garden soils. Newer releases like the aptly named Afterburner ('David Odom') maintain that symmetry while underscoring the species' ember-glowing, almost-too-hot-to-touch fall

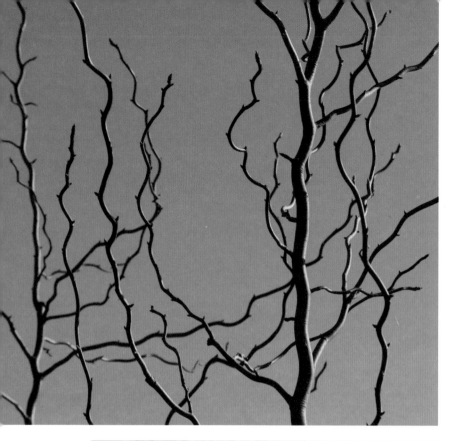

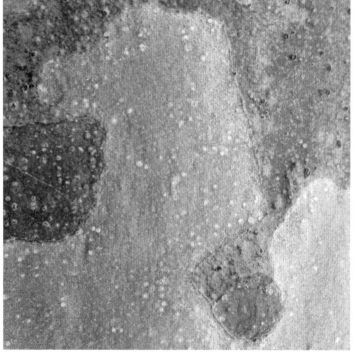

(clockwise from top left)

Nyssa sylvatica 'Zydeco Twist', elegantly etching the coldest winter sky.

Paperbark maple (*Acer griseum*).

Lacebark pine (*Pinus bungeana*).

color. *Nyssa sylvatica* 'Zydeco Twist', discovered by Sherwood Akin in Louisiana, puts a twist on all this neatly limbed architecture. It's not exactly contorted, though its zigzagging trunks and branches offer a delightfully repetitious dance of lines. Against a blue winter sky, it's the stuff of art galleries. In summer, its quirky personality gets cloaked in layers of high-gloss foliage.

ALL BARK AND NO BITE

Some trees are all bark and no bite. Bark is like the wallpaper of the garden, always present even when the room is bare. But bark has no bite, mostly because horticulturists shy away from talking about it, afraid this nerdy self-indulgence might scare people. But bark is just too cool to go quiet about—it's shaggy, it's flaky, it's corky, it's blocky. It's at once impenetrable armor and a delicate coat, easily injured if you engage in too much arboricultural roughhousing. A series of trees planted for their bark alone makes any garden in the off-season a delightful place to stroll.

A trio of Asian natives tops my list of barky favorites, starting with paperbark maple (*Acer griseum*), introduced from the forests of China by E. H. Wilson, one of America's most storied plant explorers. As a shade tree, it's a slow investment, eventually topping out at thirty feet, if you're around to see it. But as a novelty piece of wooden sculpture, you can enjoy it for its bark from the first day you plant it. Like many plants, it's a conversation kickstarter, the kind of plant that seems to murmur ethereally to even the least interested and suggest a talking point. It's worth touching, too, its shaggy curls flaking off into something resembling fine Chinese parchments. In a word—refined.

Another highly regarded Chinese tree in the American landscape is lacebark pine (*Pinus bungeana*), adored for its exfoliating camouflage up and down thirty- to forty-foot-tall trunks. The finest specimens grow into multi-stemmed islands worth blending into the landscape, but beware the cost of time. It takes up to ten years for specimens to develop the bark that buckles my knees, a worthwhile wait for years of unending pleasure.

Climbing the trunk of a Japanese pagodatree (*Sophora japonica*) would require a little more effort than the previous two species. At more than sixty feet tall, the broad, overarching canopy fills out to form an impressive outline against the horizon. The tree doesn't earn much respect from hardcore shade tree proponents, who blame it for its messiness and weak habit, neither of which points I entirely dispute; but when sited appropriately, decades-old specimens are easy to enjoy for their profusion of pendent, creamy flowers in spring followed by string-of-pearls fruits later in the summer, and if limbs are protected from winter winds, breakage is minimal. In winter, the tree's slate gray bark with interlacing ridges looks like a well-worn Perry Ellis blazer.

Acer palmatum 'Bihou'.

(left) Japanese pagodatree (*Sophora japonica*).

Who doesn't want a well-worn if a slightly wrinkled Perry Ellis blazer in their midwinter garden? Yes, this tree has style and is tolerant of poor air quality, too.

Hardly runners up, I'd be remiss not to shout a few words of praise for the untold hundreds of Japanese maple (*Acer palmatum*) cultivars with various shades of bark, sultry to stunning. 'Bihou' bewitched me when I first saw its coral limbs in February—there's nothing tepid about its twigs, which look great glowing in the landscape or in the close confines of some super-large container right off the doorstep.

Bringing the discussion closer to home, yellow birch (*Betula alleghaniensis*) has a lot going for it, chiefly its yellow fall color and bark (at least on younger trees) that rivals the finest bronze and copper foil. It peels and exfoliates, revealing a rough hewn and brawny trunk whose angled, efferent branches ably frame views into other parts of the garden. Plus, this birch is mostly resistant to the plague of the bronze birch borer and is not abundant in gardens, a double whammy for anyone looking to turn a few heads in the neighborhood. Across the Atlantic, an Asian counterpart, Chinese red birch (*B. albosinensis* var. *septentrionalis*), basks in the limelight of horticultural popularity thanks to its unusually sea green summer foliage and peeling, pink and cinnamon bark. Oddly though, it's remarkably absent from American gardens, which is a total bummer. Somebody should fix this.

Yellow birch (*Betula alleghaniensis*).

But if you're really looking to go native with a plant nobody has heard of, why not try *Leitneria floridana*, the strangely tropical-looking but entirely hardy shrub known as corkwood? Now this isn't just something weird for the sake of being weird (I have several plants to share from that list, if you're so inclined). This plant has real merits, even it's not flashy. It forms twiggy, suckering groves that withstand wet soils and prevent erosion, and its lanky stems look like they're wrought from the finest slate. Bizarre, willow-esque, burnt brown catkins appear in March long before the leaves unfurl. A grove grew outside my office at Iowa State University, throughout my time there as a graduate student. I took an interest in them after watching them travel the ornamental orbit—from catkins, through to leafing out and yellow fall color, and finally to naked stems; it was one of the backburner projects in my lab. These plants are rare in the wild and almost unheard of in the nursery trade but deserve a wider audience. Let's rally.

Overlapping the shrub-tree category, seven-son flower (*Heptacodium miconioides*), the novelty Chinese native coveted as a specimen by arboretums and plant collectors, is rarely praised for its shaggy, peeling bark. Plant geeks go nuts for its clouds of white flowers in August, followed by fruits and leftover flower parts (sepal-like calyces, as botanists call them) that are easily confused for flowers themselves. They gleam in bright rosy red shades, catching notice when they might otherwise have

Styrax japonicus 'Pink Chimes'.

(opposite) The leftover floral receptacles of seven-son flower (*Heptacodium miconioides*), which easily pass for Flowers Part Deux after the white rosettes have faded.

been ignored. The bark, though, gets recognized only when someone has done some clever pruning, limbing up the branches so that the canopy fills into an oval above, revealing ruggedly barky stems to anyone below. This style of pruning reveals the tree's muscular armature and makes it a desirable structural element in gardens large or small.

BELLS AND CHIMES

Why snowbell trees aren't more common puzzles me. Their flowers look like snowy white bells—ding, dong, ding—what could be better? As a group, they prefer slightly acidic soil, which does limit their sustainability in gardens with high pH soils. The genus isn't small and is largely unexplored—almost 130 species populate the ranks of the family tree, but only a half-dozen or so species commonly make their way into Western horticulture. Four species are native to the United States, including *Styrax americanus*, a modest small tree or small-framed shrub. I grow Kankakee, a form distributed commercially from collections at the northernmost population, near the Illinois town of that name. It's a charmer, even if it slowly starts to hate life in my pH 7.5 soil by the close of the summer (only to repeat the sequence every year: eternal sunshine of the horticultural mind).

Tree breeders have wisely placed bets that more snowbells will be sensationalized, introducing a flurry of new varieties with distinctive habits and descriptive cultivar names (an unusual circumstance in today's world). All in all, variable habits aside, these are some of the best small-statured trees, rarely growing more than thirty feet tall. I'm most smitten with Snowcone and 'Fragrant Fountain', which couldn't be more different. Snowcone basically looks like it sounds, a broadly pyramidal tree topping out into a fat, rounded crown befitting its name. 'Fragrant Fountain' spills its abundant floral display from atop a five-foot-tall tree that grows just as wide. Nothing says spring more than a robe of snowbells draping to the ground, right? And in one notable instance, a snowbell tree is not white-flowered but rather pink (please no yellow snowbells); enter *Styrax japonicus* 'Pink Chimes', which is a personal favorite, even if the buds are actually pinker than the flowers themselves. Marleys Pink Parasol ('JLWeeping'), a new introduction, offers charming promise for both pink flowers and weeping habit.

Pterostyrax hispidus, a relative of snowbell trees, is a fine tree, reaching twenty-five feet tall and more at maturity in almost any kind of soil. It graces the garden in midsummer with nine-inch-long combs of flowers that look as if they've been uncorked from a bottle of Champagne. Fizzy bubbles, anyone? Yellow fall color makes nearly four seasons of impact—flowers to fall color to form.

Carolina silverbell (*Halesia carolina*, syn. *H. tetraptera*) has had all kinds of name problems. Regardless of your nomenclatural stance, two

Pterostyrax hispidus.

absolutes underscore the horticultural merits of this underappreciated bell-flowered tree. First, it's a southeastern native but isn't totally inept in northern climates, mustering the courage to flower in protected sites as far north as zone 4. Second, read everything about *Styrax* and apply accordingly—pH tolerance, size and habit, flowering time, and landscape context.

Speaking of chimes, fringetrees (*Chionanthus*) come to mind. Three words—fringy, rare, awesome. What was formerly a group of highly regarded native trees has slipped round to the low point of the botanical clock and for some reason, increasingly, the evolutionary one as well. These American natives are becoming rarer and rarer, disappearing from their swampland homes scattered throughout the Southeast, possibly victims of the emerald ash borer scourge. Happily, as landscape plants, swamps are not a prerequisite for these beauties. In fact, fringetrees are quite tolerant of drought, an insight not entirely surprising given that swamps are usually wettest during spring, only to dry out later in the year. In full bloom, few things can steal a fringetree's thunder—silvery, puffy clouds of flowers in shimmerous showers.

Each spring, our landscapes are full of purple smoky blights (otherwise known as *Cotinus coggygria*). How I wish we saw more of our native smoketree, *C. obovatus*. With a scattered distribution in the wild including central Texas, the Ouachita Mountains, and southern Tennessee, this is one of the best native American trees for fall color. It burns the eyes in amber, pink, red, and orange shades, often on the same plant, a volcanic storm of fiery colors borne in an irregular, amorphous canopy some twenty to thirty feet above the ground. In summer, it's familiarly a smoketree, except that the usual cloying purple clouds are replaced with hazy pink. No offense to Jimi Hendrix, but pink haze is a lot sexier than purple haze.

(clockwise from top)

Carolina silverbell (*Halesia carolina*).

American smoketree (*Cotinus obovatus*)
in autumn color.

American fringetree (*Chionanthus virginicus*).

SHRUBS

No, not Bushes, not presidents. Shrubs. As a horticulturist, this one actually bugs me a little. I'm guilty of letting "dirt" slide for "soil," but "bushes" semantically substituting for "shrubs"? Them's fighting words. Let's agree to depoliticize the garden and call these wonderful woodies what they are—shrubs. Shrubs come in all sizes and shapes and can potentially satisfy any gardener's needs. Prior to their renaissance in the last two decades, shrubs fell into two categories—hellish hedges and scraggly benchwarmers. Hellish hedges needed constant maintenance and never really pleased anyone with a creative mind, unless you were neurotic enough to shape them with hedge trimmers once a week. Scraggly benchwarmers were the sorts of overgrown, unkempt explosions of twigs that populated the back fences and side yards of our

upbringing. Once in a decade, someone would go on a tear, hack them to the ground, and have a beer in the aftermath. We've come a long way, since.

IN THE SPOTLIGHT

Shrubs nowadays earn the spotlight—whole gardens are constructed around their charms. They require less maintenance than highly populated perennial beds and are more tempered in their contributions to the yearlong garden aesthetic. Consider *Sorbaria sorbifolia* 'Sem', the shrub with a moniker that sounds like a nickname you'd give your best childhood friend. Until 'Sem', there wasn't much to write home about, where the species was concerned. A plant of muted ornamental value, the wild types form a suckering clump that can spread up to ten feet wide and about half as tall; flowers are reasonably interesting, a plumed twist on common spirea, earning it the common name false spirea. But this shrub, native to Kazakhstan, is brutishly tough, hardy to zone 2. Enter 'Sem', the Dutch-born hybrid of two unnamed selections of the species, a chic up-do with salon-quality bronze and red highlights in early spring as its feathery leaves unfurl. As it grows, that metallic blend gives way to neon green—a designer color combo brought to you by ingenious plant selection. As a hedge, it's a shiner. As a focal point, it's arresting. In a large container, it's all thrills. Why this plant hasn't gained more traction to date remains a mystery—you *all* need one.

Mention shrubs gaining traction, and I'm obliged to mention *Mahonia*. With more and more species in this genus earning appreciation and new cultivars turning consumer heads, these new-age barberry and epimedium relatives have merits galore beyond the familiar Oregon grape holly (*M. aquifolium*). In the foliage-for-connoisseurs department, *M. gracilipes* and *M. eurybracteata* rule supreme. It sounds a bit naughty to say, but I love *M. gracilipes* for its chalky undersides. Add flowers to the ensemble, and it makes for botanical burlesque. Easy to grow with few requirements beyond light shade, this deer-resistant shrub maintains urban proportions in the neighborhood of four to six feet with free-spirited branching that's informal but not unkempt. The flowers remind me of a tequila sunrise, orange blending into pink and back again on the surface of sprite, outward-facing cups.

A newer release, *Mahonia eurybracteata* 'Soft Caress', makes a strong case for the value of handsome, wonderfully silky leaves in the modern landscape. In zone 7 and above, it's a cinch for drought-tolerance and easy care, provided afternoon shade. In northerly climates, you'll have to resort to container culture and go to an unbelievable amount of work to keep a plant alive in your garage through the winter. But what's serious gardening without a little crazy?

Mahonia fremontii is a superb medium-sized shrub for Western landscapes with silver foliage overlaid with aquamarine and

Mahonia fremontii.

(left) Bottlebrush buckeye (*Aesculus parviflora*) leaves in autumn colors.

branch-engulfing clouds of golden sulfureous flowers in mid-spring. This drought-tolerant shrub's fruiting display rivals its flowers for interest and attention—pudgy, cherry-colored drupes populate its twiggy proportions well into autumn. With a little pruning, it shapes into a comely head-turner in xeric zones.

Also on the highly desirable and necessary list is bottlebrush buckeye (*Aesculus parviflora*), a bushy buckeye native to the southeastern United States. In June and July, after most shrubs have settled into summer growth, these aptly named, multi-stemmed shrubs of towering proportions rocket into flower, laden with nectar and calling out to butterflies for miles. They thrive in a variety of soils and in bright to filtered exposures, which makes them perfect structural specimens for smaller landscapes. 'Rogers' blooms later, with even larger flowers than normal—how big do flowers in your garden have to be, anyway? In autumn, the shrub proves it's no one-hit wonder, outdoing its garden neighbors with striking golden fall color, displayed on palmate, umbrella-shaped leaves.

And now for something completely different. My master's work in college focused on an obscure shrub that even the botanical cognoscenti gave me flack for—eastern leatherwood (*Dirca palustris*). *Dirca* holds the bastard stepchildren of the daphne family (Thymelaeaceae). In a family replete with epic, decadently scented show plants, it seems out of place. Yet to me, it's the epitome of stylish and sublime in one plant. One thing to remember about chic plants and hip gardeners—the elements of garden style sometimes aren't the flashiest, and intentionally so. Think about the little votive candles on a mantel or tabletop. Though they are small and insignificant, that mantel would look a lot less magical during the holiday season without them. Plants are the same way. Crafting a stylish garden that looks, feels, and grows like you comes down to embracing all the plant world has to offer—flashy to subdued. In that way, *D. palustris* deserves a spot in every shady nook spanning its easterly North American range—from Bangor (Maine) to Bettendorf (Iowa).

If you're not convinced yet, *Dirca palustris* takes the prize for being one of the earliest shrubs to flower in the northern temperate landscape, sporting dangling yellow flowers in concert with the woodland garden's ephemeral chorus—hepaticas, merryworts (*Uvularia*), and claytonias. Broadly adaptable to a variety of pH conditions, this slow-growing shrub teaches gardeners to savor the experience of watching a few-leaved seedling age into an arborescent shrub, much as a vintner savors the aging of a fine Merlot. And what does a leatherwood have on a Merlot? Yellow fall color, grandly so.

Sweetshrubs (*Calycanthus*) aren't exactly mainstream commodities either, though that unfortunate attitude needs to change. I mean, they aren't half as obscure as *Dirca*, but you might be fooled into thinking that, given their overall absence from American gardens. As a whole, they make great background shrubs, reaching heights of five to nine feet and more, and often half as a wide. The flowers are intriguing, if somewhat peculiar. I remember an excellent specimen of *C. floridus*, well grown and thriving outside my office in graduate school. There, at the northern extent of its growing range, I witnessed its spring ritual—bevies of spicily scented flowers in chestnut shades, looking more like nuts than flowers. It's a free-spirited sucker(er), colonizing (once situated) moister soils reminiscent of its woodland bottomland haunts throughout the southeastern United States. And it's hardier than you might think, growing and flowering reliably in zone 5.

The story of *Calycanthus* 'Venus' is the kind of horticultural breeding epic that gives me goosebumps. The intrepid Tom Ranney at North Carolina State University sought to reinvent sweetshrubs, crossing *C. floridus*, *C. occidentalis*, and *C. chinensis* (formerly *Sinocalycanthus chinensis* and the progenitor of the famous 'Hartlage Wine') to arrive at 'Venus', a zestily fragrant hybrid that is officially rated as hardy to zone 6.

FLUTTERING

With all the buzz around butterfly bushes (no pun about the Buzz series intended), it's hard to narrow down a half-dozen to cover succinctly. Growing up, I had tepid interest in these butterfly magnets, mostly due to their half-hardy reputation. I wasn't alone: many northern gardeners were disappointed by lackluster returns in the year or two after planting. Either as a result of smarter selection or warming climate, that opinion seems to have been washed away in the flood of new varieties coming onto the market. Gardeners still have reason to be leery, though. Many early selections of *Buddleja davidii* have made themselves remarkably "at home" on both coasts, taking advantage of warmer winters in recent decades to become obnoxious, almost noxious, and even banned from sale in some states. The research doesn't hold that the whole genus should be held responsible for the seediness of one or a few species; modern cultivars are borderline sterile.

Some lesser-known butterfly bushes, among dozens of unheard-of species in a genus with almost a hundred members and probably as many cultivars, populate a roster that reads like King Arthur's entourage in a Monty Python sketch: the silver, drooping *Buddleja nivea* var. *yunnanensis*, the honeydipper flowers of 'Honeycomb', the woolly *B. marrubiifolia*, and the weeping, underappreciated *B. lindleyana*, among others.

Buddleja nivea var. *yunnanensis* is here to prove a plant can be compared to Eeyore and still be desirable. It's big (think Paul Bunyon big: almost twelve feet tall), gray, and droopy, in the best ways possible, with pendulous panicles of tiny purple flowers, reminiscent of oversized lamb's ears (*Stachys byzantina*), cascading in goosy contortions

An established *Calycanthus* 'Venus' at Arrowhead Alpines nursery in Michigan.

(top) Eastern leatherwood (*Dirca palustris*) with firefly flowers abuzz in early April.

(right) Carolina allspice (*Calycanthus floridus*) is a stemmy shrub with enthusiastic floral displays and noteworthy fall color.

Buddleja nivea var. *yunnanensis* droops its silver fuzzy leaves.

in midair. Among the hardiest of butterfly bushes, these shrubs will weather through zone 6 winters with some dieback. But here's the thing—even when they've died back, the emerging new growth offers the bonus of being exceptionally fuzzy, covered in soft gray hairs that beg to be touched. While some might consider this too nerdy to bear, irresistibly touchy-feely foliage *and* structural height together make this plant a special addition to the garden's backdrop.

Truth be told, silver buddlejas aren't exactly uncommon. *Buddleja* 'Lochinch' is a hybrid between the silver-felted *B. fallowiana* and the common *B. davidii*. The foliage offers plenty of interest until twelve-inch candles of purple flowers steal the show from summer into fall. *Buddleja fallowiana* is slightly more tender than *B. davidii*, which tends to show through in its derivative cultivars. 'Lochinch', a stout dwarf measuring four to five feet tall and wide, is borderline hardy in zone 5, and successful cultivation probably hinges a lot on careful siting of individual plants.

Yellow and orange are abundant in the butterfly bush clan, which is welcome news to anyone fatigued by the overabundance of blue and purple in gardens. Orangest to my eye is *Buddleja marrubiifolia*, a desert native of southwest Texas and northwest Mexico that's picking up traction in buzz circles. As a landscape specimen, this drought-tolerant dynamo offers marmalade flowers that positively pop against fuzzy,

Buddleja alternifolia.

stainless steel leaves. Starve it of water, and the leaves get more silvery and fuzzy—the ideal payoff for neglectful gardening. But its lack of hardiness limits its widespread use beyond containers in any garden colder than zone 8. Alternatively, 'Honeycomb' has Georgia upbringings, coming out of Michael Dirr's breeding work at University of Georgia, but is hardy to zone 5 and an elegant flowerer. This deer-proof hybrid sports amber flowers from June to frost in four- to six-inch-long panicles, on stems that are ultimately capable of reaching five to six feet, depending on the length of summer.

Weeping. Underappreciated. *Buddleja lindleyana* is a descending, rambling, summer-flowering butterfly bush that takes on whatever personality the gardener wants, given a little training and influence. Limbed up, it's a fountain of awesomeness with overflowing purple-aging-blue flowers. Left to its own devices, it stays closer to ground, with scrambling stems serendipitously mingling throughout the garden. Mingle as it may, it emits a sweet, subtle fragrance much like common butterfly bush (*B. davidii*).

Sulking in similar obscurity, *Buddleja alternifolia* is a zone-5-hardy butterfly bush that doesn't need cutting back in spring—it flowers on old wood and usually in mid-spring, a decadent lavender surprise in a season that isn't used to butterfly bushes.

VIBURNUMS

If there are two things that go together like cookies and milk, it's viburnums and Michael Dirr, retired University of Georgia horticulture professor and leading woody plant authority. In fact it was Dirr himself who wrote, "A garden without viburnums is like a life without the pleasures of music and art." He forgot to name chocolate, explicitly, but we'll include that as art. His sentiment is otherwise spot-on, and I'm almost ashamed to attempt appraisals here, tempted to just skip the whole lot in favor of assigning his monograph on the genus as required reading.

On a theme of the earliest—there's something to be said for being first—*Viburnum farreri* is essential, even if in northern climes it's subject to the chilly, nippy nights of early (barely) spring. But the joy you get from watching the buds transform from tightly clasped appleblossoms to delicate white pom-poms is surely worth the gamble. Here's how to turn the odds in your favor: rather than planting early flowering shrubs against a warm, southerly exposure, tuck them inside a walled garden or against a shaded corner of the house to delay flowering. It seems counterintuitive, but placing these "tender" budded shrubs in cold spots actually ensures that they bloom when temperatures moderate, slowing down their physiology until warmer temperatures ensue.

On the completely opposite end of the spectrum, *Viburnum sieboldii* 'Wavecrest' is grown for its fall color, albeit by fewer people than it ought to be. Named and introduced by Iowa nurseryman Eugene Coffman, 'Wavecrest' is a noteworthy selection of the otherwise coarsely textured Siebold viburnum, which is doggedly hardy to the chilly depths of zone 4. Boasting bright, rusty red fall color and fruits on a similar theme, 'Wavecrest' can reach small tree-like proportions at twelve to fifteen feet tall and doesn't look half bad grown as one. The new emerging leaf buds in the spring belie the season, harkening to the ruddy colors expected in autumn. White flowers frost terminal stems in midsummer.

Not all viburnums earn high marks for hardiness, and gardeners in southerly parts reap the benefits. Favored among the glossy, broadleaf evergreen viburnums is the variegated form of *Viburnum japonicum*. Handsome as a rounded hedge or a boxy specimen, *V. japonicum* 'Variegatum' earns its street cred from dappled yellow-on-green leaves alone, its flowers and fruits an added but unnecessary bonus. Regular forms of the species, though, are no duds. White clusters of remarkably fragrant flowers span nearly five inches in diameter, a guaranteed treat on a rare shrub that prefers light shade from blistering southern suns and shelter from desiccating winter winds.

Viburnum plicatum 'Popcorn' is a prince among its kind and a fine shrub for gardens in zone 5 and above, with a reputation for avalanches of snowy white flowers in mid- to late spring. Dirr counts it among the best, most notably for its superb heat and drought tolerance.

(opposite top) *Viburnum farreri*.

(opposite bottom) *Viburnum plicatum* 'Popcorn'.

Vernonia baldwinii 'Border Crossing'.

BIG AND HERBACEOUS

There are some plants that just seem like big comfy chairs, the kind of oversized furniture perfect for snuggling down into and keeping forever. Big, tall, husky perennials are handsome staples to be planted in spaces where they liven up the garden party. But there is an art to craftily installing them. They are statement plants after all—big statements—and like every seasoned politician knows, a big statement may not always be received as it was intended. If you're looking to totally block off the view of your house from neighbors or anyone else peering from the outside in, there are plenty of house-engulfing solutions—cue the blooper roll of outsized Leyland cypresses and poorly pruned trees. Assuming you're hoping to avoid a blunder, here are some bodacious perennials you can't go wrong with.

IRONCLAD

The ironweeds (*Vernonia*) bring a certain punk quality to the landscape. It's something about their common name—they are tough, rugged, and all-around hardcore. With purple flowers in the dead of the blazing, blistering summer, these stalwart natives call out for attention like that emo chick with the tie-dye hairdo. Like it or not, she made you look. Plus, ironweeds do her one better—they tend to get big and blousy, which is not a polite way of saying drunk and disorderly. Gardeners have no time for unnecessary staking, so plants that can't keep their sea legs might as well stay at the nursery and live off the hose. The biggest of all the ironweeds out there is probably Tony Avent's 'Jonesboro Giant', a selection of *V. gigantea* with a solid reputation for ten- to twelve-foot-tall, windproof stems. In other words, she won't fall down. However, if your garden's profile is more in line structurally with the church steeple in the suburbs than the skyscraper downtown, you might want to consider the equally lovely *V. baldwinii* (Baldwin's ironweed) or *V. noveboracensis* (New York ironweed), both of which often average out at five feet. Size and color aside, these three ironweeds share an affinity for sunny exposures and wet feet (think peripheries of rain gardens, adjacent to the south-side downspout, or the inevitable ditch), though if a drought sets in, they'll tough it out; they're not called ironweeds for nothing.

I collected a dwarf form of *Vernonia baldwinii*, flowering at only eighteen inches tall, alongside an old highway near the Iowa-Missouri line. In the garden the following season, this drought-tolerant butterfly magnet quickly attained some size though it remained boxy in habit—enough for me to continue to regard it as a nicer selection than most. Its grayed amethyst flowers seem charged for an early unfurling but then dither from bud to blossom, arriving just in time to inaugurate high summer. I named this form 'Border Crossing'. Stay tuned.

As a sidebar to this large and in-charge section—there are ironweeds that don't rocket to lofty proportions but deserve as much garden attention as those that do. Notably, *Vernonia lettermannii* has earned considerable praise for its feathery fine foliage, purple-pink star-dusted flowers, and ability to thrive in hellstrips and awful soils. Hailing from rocky, hot hillsides in the Ouachita Basin of Arkansas, you'd think at first this was an amsonia: its foliage fools even the most astute plant geeks, and its size makes the proposition all the more plausible. But come August, it shows its true colors, literally, erupting into a cloud of flowers that calls every passing butterfly for miles. 'Iron Butterfly' is the only named selection—a nicely architected, compact form of the species. Take heed of its native condition—plants in the wild stressed by less-than-ideal soils are less likely to grow as rapidly or robustly as those grown under garden conditions. With even a little extra water, they may want to flop, not because they are bad plants, but because of too much aqua viva. Plant under dry conditions or alongside something that it can flop into.

PRAIRIE SPIRES

Until recently, Culver's root (*Veronicastrum virginicum*), despite its many charms, just didn't have much to offer in a crowded plant market of blowsy standouts. But then a quartet of cultivars came along: 'Adoration', 'Apollo', 'Erica', and 'Fascination'. These pinkish- and reddish-flowered babes quite frankly rock my socks off, though I still have a soft spot for the white-flowered native strains I encountered in roadside ditches on drives and walks around my rural homeland. Stylistically, think of them as scaffolds—clay-tolerant skyscrapers that visually define the rest of the garden. Tall plants like these, though not in flower until late summer, provide solid foundation for shorter, clumping plants throughout the border. In my clay garden (yes, I'm that guy that gets excited about clay soil), I have Culver's root interspersed with various mid-size miscanthus and underplanted with *Helenium* 'Sahin's Early Flowerer', daylilies, and Korean burnet (*Sanguisorba hakusanensis*), for a headlining show of texture and whimsy.

A list of prairie spires wouldn't be complete without mentioning rosinweeds and compass plants, members of the genus *Silphium*. To many, they are just ADYCs—botanical slang for "another damn yellow composite." And while they *are* yellow daisies, they are essential yellow daisies for the late-season garden. Picking five species to talk about verges on excessively discriminating, even in a genus with yellow flowers (with only one exception—the white-flowering *S. albiflorum*, which is so rare in the trade, it's barely worth the tease).

Towering above the prairie sea at more than ten feet in height at peak bloom, prairie dock (*Silphium terebinthinaceum*) well represents this genus of ruggedly durable plants with often profoundly deep root

Culver's root (*Veronicastrum virginicum*) stands tall in garden borders where it gets decent moisture and bright light. Tough, dependable, and effortless, it's a prime American native to bear the brunt of summer.

systems—the husky taproots of prairie dock are nearly as long as its flower stems are tall. Taprooted plants have evolved these subterranean structures in order to thrive. By mining out water and nutrients below the normal planes of competition, these plants survive adverse conditions in style. I grow prairie dock in what I jokingly call black clay, the deceptively colored vein of gluey, nutrient-rich soil that runs through my garden. To the eye, it looks like black gold. To the touch, it's the stuff potters dream of. My own wretched dirt aside, calling prairie dock striking is an understatement. Not only is it big, its foliage brings a titanic dose of texture and contrast to a vignette with the catmints (*Nepeta*) and a row of ninebarks (*Physocarpus opulifolius* 'Diablo') in its vicinity. In flower, during the inferno of mid- and late summer, it's a positive pennant with widely spaced branches of yellow daisies. Staking? Don't bother. These flower stalks might make saplings jealous but never push the boundaries of coarseness, in spite of their lumbering tallness.

Among other silphiums that border on coarse and lumbering but merit planting are compass plant (*Silphium laciniatum*) and cup plant (*S. perfoliatum*), both with storied vernacular names in the romanticized tales of pioneers settling the prairie. Both tell practical stories. It's true that compass plant does track the sun throughout the day, a truly eccentric attribute, and cup plant does collect water in the basin formed at the intersection of its leaves and stems. In even average garden soil, compass plants can stretch to ridiculous heights, so consider limiting them by letting them fight it out with other plants or staging them so that everything doesn't go tumbling down. Until recently, I looked down on cup plants as good garden plants, even if I respected them in the wild. Then Brent Horvath, plant breeder and owner of Intrinsic Perennial Gardens in Hebron, Illinois, introduced 'The Holy Grail'—a golden-leaved collected form that could force a complete rewrite of the famed Monty Python flick if word gets around. In the spring, acid chartreuse leaves rise from the ground to my annual surprise—the sight is that arresting. By midsummer, the neon fades but the awesome remains. In full flower at six feet tall, there's no arguing that this diva owns the scene.

Rosinweeds (*Silphium integrifolium*) are some of the most underused silphiums—the most overlooked of the overlooked. Starkly textural, tough, and hardy, these Central Plains perennials laugh in the face of high summer, bringing much needed color to an otherwise tired, not to say scorched garden scene. I believe strongly that some seasons of the year have a just-so kind of look—and for August, that look is blended yellow and gold against clear blue skies. Rosinweed loves a bright, open exposure and tolerates a range of soils, much as its close relative whorled rosinweed (*S. trifoliatum*) does. Talk about a plant nobody grows, visitors to my garden in July often gaze heavenward in awe at the array of yellow stars that dot the ends of rigid, reddish stems.

The aster family isn't known for its fidelity. This wild-occurring hybrid between *Silphium perfoliatum* and *S. integrifolium* seems to have the best of both worlds for a flower that's *still* only yellow.

Whorled rosinweed (*Silphium trifoliatum*).

Even when not in full flower, the remnants are entertaining, the perfect plant for planting alongside the firepit for a post-barbecue, ale-induced discussion about native plants and why they ever need to grow *this* tall.

HOLLYHOCKS, ETC.

Next to the Big and Tall Botanical Boutique in my garden, you'll find Hollyhocks, Etc. It's no secret that I'm seriously addicted to these biggish biennials (and perennials) of cottage border fame. I've fiddled with crossing them for more than a decade, since I was a mere boy with absolutely no conscious clue of what I was doing other than selecting the prettiest of the bunches I grew. But breeding hollyhocks is a lot like herding cats—any advances made inevitably veer off in random directions, all away from the intended goal. I always chuckle when I come across a fellow gardener who hybridizes hollyhocks (um, it's happened exactly once). It's kind of like catching a glimpse of yourself in a mirror and laughing at your own outfit (what the hell were we thinking?).

But the world of hollyhocks (*Alcea*) isn't entirely laughable. In fact, of the nearly sixty species distributed throughout eastern Europe and Asia Minor, several are true, disease-resistant perennials with wildflowery personalities. Chiefly *A. rugosa* comes to mind, the variably tinted acid yellow and green hollyhock of perennial virtue. I was enamored of it when I was thirteen, impressed that a hollyhock could come in colors other than the boring pastel pinks and reds I'd inherited in the

×Alcalthaea suffrutescens 'Parkallee'.

farmstead garden of my youth. As hollyhocks go, it's a doer, forming hunky clumps with multiple stems offering countless dozens of flowers throughout midsummer, the perfect background plant to busier floral scenes in the foreground. Watch out for the seedlings, too. They'll bloom in shades of their parent, creamy to green, yellowy to near white.

Alceaholicism doesn't end there. In 1953, Hungarian plant breeder Zoltan Kovats made a series of novel, fascinating crosses between the common marshmallow (*Althaea officinalis*) and hollyhock (*Alcea rosea*). The result was the hybrids of ×*Alcalthaea suffrutescens*—'Parkallee', 'Parkrondell', 'Parkfrieden', and 'Parktraum'. Of the four, 'Parkallee' and 'Parkrondell' seem to be the most available, and my experience with 'Parkallee' motivates me to find and grow the rest. The semi-double flowers are intermediate between a hollyhock and a marshmallow in appearance, with tufted creamy petaloids subtending clusters of purple anthers. Though sterile, these intergeneric hybrids offer everything a gardener wants in a hollyhock: they are highly tolerant of hollyhock rust, suffer little from nibbling summer insects, and bloom virtually nonstop from the end of June through and after frost on six- to eight-foot-tall stems arranged like a vase emerging from the ground. Totes cool.

Large-flowered wild hollyhock (*Iliamna grandiflora*) doesn't really sound like a hollyhock if you're used to hearing *Alcea rosea* roll off the tongue. But this genus of "wild hollyhocks" calls various parts of western North America home (with the exception of eastern disjunct populations of *I. rivularis*, riverside wild hollyhock, which occur in Illinois and Virginia). Little is known about these species in cultivation, and they are barely available commercially. Ellen Hornig, former proprietor of the now-shuttered Seneca Hill Perennials, was one of the few sources around when the genus came to my attention years ago. *Iliamna grandiflora* grows about three feet tall and sports white, typical hollyhock-esque flowers almost nonstop from spring through summer. The best part (and why it's of interest to anyone dabbling in hollyhock sex): it's mostly resistant to hollyhock rust. Mostly. These aren't your grandmother's hollyhocks, but they flower longer and more effusively than traditional hollyhocks. The first few seasons I grew them, both *I. grandiflora* and *I. rivularis* bloomed for almost four months. What typical hollyhock does that? These are the kinds of plants that deserve praise and chatter—plants that truly make gardening a rewarding experience in all seasons.

IN THE CLOUDS

Perhaps it's only the one-letter difference, but I so often associate the word "angelica" with Angelina Jolie. She should be flattered. These divas of the garden bring star-power geometry to almost any assembly. Like three sisters, they have more in common than not, but each stands alone as a powerhouse plant. Important to note, angelicas are short-lived perennials, flirting with biennialism (which is surely not as terminal as it sounds). Whether they bloom the first year or not, once they do, you'll enjoy their company for many seasons thanks to reseeding. In rich soils (which isn't a requirement for growing them successfully), they can occasionally become a bit unwieldy, at which point you just share the gospel of Angelina, er *Angelica*. Brad won't mind.

Angelica gigas is the moodiest of these three graces. Luscious, lacquered purple stems terminate in domes of the same color—alien satellites orbiting the herbaceous border. Its foliage is bold, reminiscent of maple leaves and tinted a dusky rouge. Similarly *A. stricta* 'Purpurea' ticks up the purple, opens up the spaceship, and launches more alien awesomeness into the space of the garden. The purple hovers in blackish hues, making for an unprecedented focal point. In fact while I can get all weak in the knees for their flowers, the foliage of angelicas is half the fun. *Angelica pachycarpa* almost earns higher marks for its extremely tropical, extremely plastic green boughs that hold up in even the steamiest days of summer. The flowers are nice, if you're of the green and white persuasion and enjoy a mildly cloying herbal perfume. Even if you're not, you have to give the punk beauty of flowers plus foliage a chance as it bursts into view in late summer. It's headturning, even if it's not your favorite. As architecture goes, a few angelicas are essential for a robust backdrop to the herbaceous border.

Large-flowered wild hollyhock (*Iliamna grandiflora*).

Angelica pachycarpa.

Meadow rues are one of those genera that make me blush. A cultivar like 'Black Stockings' underscores the seductress qualities of these members of the buttercup family—six-foot-tall jet black stems terminating in candy pink flowers are the botanical equivalent of a cat call. Tall, long-legged and striking could well sum up this group of perennials that know how to command attention, raising heads to a dimension of the garden so often ignored. *Thalictrum delavayi* has some of the most profound flowers of the bunch, size queens in vibrant shades of pink, purple, and even chaste white. 'Hewitt's Double' is a double form of considerable merit with six-foot-tall stems ending in purple pom-poms. The blonde of the bunch, *T. flavum*, first caught my attention with its five-foot-tall, sulfur-rising sprays in Denver Botanic Gardens shortly after I graduated high school—enchanting, to say the least. 'Illuminator', a chartreuse variety, continues to grow in my garden, less for its stature than its lime emergent foliage, which goes on to complement aureolin flowers in midsummer as it ages to aquamarine. Someone ought to write a pocket guide to meadow rues, as there's much more to say. And I will.

Thalictrum rochebrunianum 'Lavender Mist', perhaps the finest representative of its species, somehow turned up in my garden. Regardless of its provenance, I love it for its out-turned, single flowers, which radiate chic colors late into the summer on tall, sturdy stems.

Thalictrum rochebrunianum 'Lavender Mist'.

(left) *Thalictrum dasycarpum*.

Thalictrum dasycarpum is a North American meadow rue with an expansive range—almost two-thirds of the continent. With such broad versatility, you'd think it would be common in cultivation, but sad to say, it's missing from too many gardens. In the wild, I often encounter plants flowering well above my six-foot-tall head; in the garden they can be more mannered and compact. Specimens in my garden rarely flower at more than four to five feet tall.

GOING UP

And now to covering surfaces, vertically speaking. Remember that significant other in college? Always hanging around, climbing all over you when you didn't return a text message right away? Clingers, climbers, ramblers, and viners are the kinds of plants worth the entanglements. What garden could grow without a rambling vine or six? Vines lift the garden to new heights, figuratively and literally. Their flowers and seeds borne ten feet in the air have a way of humbling the garden below, and persistent stems in late winter, absent any foliage from the season before, offer a twiggy net to catch interest. Some gardeners hem vines in, straightening their lacy tendrils onto trellises and formal structures, defying gravity, bent on gardening up. If you're like me, though, you're a little less inclined to bound nature with hard structure. In any case,

Parthenocissus quinquefolia 'Monham' (Star Showers).

maximizing vertical space is a keen talent and at times a pragmatic one, particularly in urban gardens with limited ground-level space.

Gardens usually have plenty of hardscapes that can benefit from botanical augmentation, and whether presented with walls, pergolas, arbors, or bamboo teepees, many plants can take leave of the ground and bound into the air. I take a lot of flak for my fondness of Virginia creeper and its thuggish cousin Boston ivy, but *Parthenocissus quinquefolia* 'Monham' (Star Showers), a splattered variegate with a smidgen less vigor and echelons more coolness, should give everyone pause. When a wall needs more than green, plant Star Showers.

LESSONS FROM THE OZARKS

Some of the honeysuckles native to the United States turn a page from the invasive reputations of their Asian cousins, the latter of which go down in history as some of the most virile of horticultural introductions. Genera like *Lonicera* are indeed dysfunctional families, with some members earning high marks and all-star praise and others boasting rap sheets and disassociating sneers. In our zeal to weed out the crooks, it's easy to look past the do-gooders not making news. Not all vines are quite so rambunctious.

Yellow honeysuckle (*Lonicera flava*) is one that deserves praise, even as I feel late to its cause. A native species throughout the southeastern

Lonicera reticulata 'Kintzley's Ghost'.

(opposite) The rambling red alternative to
Lonicera flava, *L. sempervirens* and its many
forms are among the finest of limbering
spring-into-summer vines.

United States and north and west to Illinois, Missouri, and eastern
Kansas, *L. flava* first caught my eye rambling across the sunny surface
of a boulder in the Ozarks, an unlikely but comely support. At the kindly
insistence of the botanist whose property I was exploring, I dug up a few
small seedlings and toted them home to my garden, where they've since
thrived. How could I ever have resisted or, worse, ignored its yellow
flowers, showy trumpets for the probing beaks of hummingbirds? What
tremendously lovely plants, so pitifully underused. The best part about
L. flava is its tendency to ramble with eloquence (a rare trait indeed)—
take note, the trellis is optional. In my garden, the extending stems
crawl over a wooden fence, covering it by late spring and early summer
with flying saucer–esque foliage. Culturally, it grows in full sun to part
shade, and survives winters as cold as zone 4b.

Lonicera sempervirens 'John Clayton' appears a tad more frequently
in gardens, but not by much. Named for an early American botanist
after its 1991 discovery on the grounds of an 18th-century church
in Gloucester, Virginia, this all-yellow variant of our native wild
honeysuckle does a trade-off with *L. flava*—its butter-toned flowers
aren't quite as vibrant as those of *L. flava*, but it bustles over a trellis
at a faster pace. If you're looking for fast and furious, opt for 'Major
Wheeler', the fiery coral-flowered honeysuckle that beats all others for
mildew-resistance and floral profusion. Its abundant flowers attract
hummingbirds, as any honeysuckle should.

In keeping with the yellowy theme of honeysuckles, I can't overlook a
rarity with Iowa roots. *Lonicera reticulata* 'Kintzley's Ghost', so named
for the eerily silver-green discs that subtend spurts of golden flowers,
is as stunning as its name would suggest. The plant's origins trace to
the greenhouses at Iowa State University, where it was discovered in
the 1880s by William "Ped" Kintzley, who propagated it and shared it
with friends and family. In 2001, the cultivar finally entered commercial production, to the acclaim of plant geeks everywhere. Long after
the flowers have disappeared, the bracts remain. The plant was a 2006
Plant Select winner for its top-notch performance in high plains and
intermountain gardens.

In the wild, many of my favorite vines get along with the twiggy assis-
tance of nearby vegetation. On one of my botanical expeditions to the
Ozarks, the low-hanging branches of a hoptree (*Ptelea trifoliata*) lent
a helping limb to the tanglesome knots of climbing milkweed (*Matelea
decipiens*). The two hundred species of climbing milkweeds—distant
relatives of the familiar butterfly weeds (*Asclepias tuberosa* and *A. syriaca*)—are virtually unknown in horticulture, a fact which should stim-
ulate your curiosity. Thirty-two of these are U.S. natives and damn cool
vines at that, in spite of their less-than-marquee personalities. *Matelea
decipiens* might well be one of the showier American species, with
satin maroon flowers arrayed in starry clusters offset by heart-shaped

leaves. The scent of the plant stirs up controversy among the handful of plant geeks who know this plant—kind of like theater geeks arguing about who played a better Mama Rose. More erudite noses detect a strong, musky fragrance, unapologetically earthy, a perfume for adult gourmands. Less sophisticated noses, like mine, think it smells like day-old oil in a deep-fat fryer, a fragrance I'm not keen on recalling. Fortunately, I rarely lean in for a sniff—if you're so inclined, I'm anxious to know what you'll think. This species chimes in again in fall, sporting yellow fall color as the leaves weather away. The perfect support for this understated vine? A bentwood trellis next to a worn-out fence needing a little vegetative accoutrement. And a warning: in light shade and cool, moist soils, this climbing milkweed could be so happy as to get a bit weedy. Look out for the closely related, otherworldly *M. gonocarpos*, a species with green flowers and black highlights.

Climbing milkweed (*Matelea decipiens*).

CLEMATIS WORTH LOVING

Trying to distill my gushing, uncontainable, effusive love for clematis into a few words borders on impossible, but here's what I've got. I tend to eschew the popular and abundant larger-flowered *Clematis* hybrids for the minimalistic, free-flowering species and small-flowered hybrids. At the top of that list are the Viornas, the American subgenus known for classic, tastemaker vines like its namesake *C. viorna* and roving *C. texensis*, which is just as true-grit tough, as any Texan would know. Volumes could and should be written about these vines; though slow-growing, they're worth the wait and pay dividends in flowers that are almost too damn cute for their own good.

If you're looking for something really special, try the bluebill (*Clematis pitcheri*) or the closely related pale leatherflower (*C. versicolor*). Pointed like a beak and cuter than a lovebird nibbling at its mate, the dainty flowers of these two cousins nod in clusters of three or more at the end of twining stems, ranging in color from felt browns to pewter blues and rarely light pinks (naturally, the most desirable color is the rarest). Both species hail roughly from the center of the country, venturing into the lower Appalachians and Mississippi and Alabama. They tolerate light shade and bloom from mid-spring through summer and sporadically into fall, mingling perfectly amid roses and shrubs as they twine their way skyward.

In the same vein, *Clematis* 'Betty Corning', a hybrid between *C. crispa* and *C. viticella*, looks finest when left to its twining devices. In floral arrangements it's a heartbreaker, but in the garden, left to amble in the company of roses or shrubs, it's a living bouquet. Some plants have a way of seducing my memory, inciting goosebumps at the recollection of a fond encounter. On a humid, dewy midsummer morning of my youth, I happened upon a garden wild with the summer and overrun with hundreds of 'Betty Corning' blooms. On a day that fairly dripped from every

Clematis 'Betty Corning'.

blade and blossom, I couldn't have imagined a finer flower to find. The secret to its success—cool roots in summer and judicious pruning in early spring. This species flowers on the current year's wood, meaning that you shouldn't leave behind the tangle tantrum from the year before. Hack it back to within a foot of the ground until you see tender, plump buds, the signs of a productive season ahead.

In contrast, some *Clematis* species flower on old wood. Take *C. chiisanensis* 'Lemon Bells', a Korean expatriate that grew up in British Columbia. A seedling selection made at the UBC Botanical Garden in 1992 from seed sent from South Korea in 1988, this handsome vine blooms in early summer and has proven hardy to zone 5 without protection. As with 'Betty Corning', success hinges on a good deal of patience, cool roots in summer, and patience. Fine vines may take a little investment, but the payoff is huge. If you've grown a clematis you know that the mantra sleep, creep, leap in some instances doesn't manifest itself in a mere three years. A few seasons ago, 'Lemon Bells' came to call a rather forlorn sand cherry (*Prunus ×cistena*) home in my garden. My dream was eventually realized—yellow lanterns hanging from red-leaved limbs (or at least distracting from the untidiness of those red-leaved limbs). A full-grown specimen of 'Lemon Bells' makes a dapper companion to nearby shrubs and large perennials, its dangling bells blending from cherry at the base to chiffon at the tips.

Clematis chiisanensis 'Lemon Bells'.

Not all clematis are grown for their flowers, though. The foliage of *Clematis recta* 'Purpurea', lusty and dusky in velvet shades, could inspire romance novels. The spring flush is as good as any purple-leaved plant you could grow, and it maintains the color well even in the heat of summer. Puffy clouds of white flowers appear in midsummer, though the plants could do without them if nature didn't dictate their appearance. Horticulturally, it's a rambler that doesn't mind part shade, supporting itself on anything from a fence post to the stems of nearby shrubs. Sometimes, it's not even worth the effort to hem it up: let it amble along through the understory until it finds a void to fill. In this sense, vines occasionally substitute as groundcovers; there's a rule breaker in every bunch. New varieties of *C. recta* only deepen the mood. Try 'Midnight Masquerade' for even more sultry leaves.

Then again, some clematis aren't grown for their seasons of foliage or flowers alone. As a token example, of which there are many, *Clematis* 'Helios', a hybrid selection of the rambunctious *C. tangutica*, maintains appearances into the fall with silky explosions of fuzzy seeds. At six to eight feet in the air, its hundreds of seed heads rival the cosmos, backlit in evening light for a final flourish. 'Helios' flowers all summer, offering an unending profusion of nodding, yellow flowers with tufts of purple stamens on current year's growth. Some say they emit the faintest scent of coconut; you'll have to nose around for yourself to confirm. If it gets

The soft-to-the-touch seed explosions of *Clematis* 'Helios' beg for interaction.

out of hand, butch it back with tough love early in the spring. If you're happy with its size, leave it alone. Judicious pruning is really a measure of a gardener's devotion. If you give a tendril the chance to twine, it will want a trellis and then the side of your house. If you have real estate to cover, you won't be displeased.

GROUND FLOOR

Then comes the cast of characters who serve a fine purpose—they cover ground, often rapidly and fashionably. These plants aren't mere fillers, though they may fill space by nature. They aren't confined to hugging the floor, though many make a habit of it. Above all, they are hallmarks of the ground, essential structural plants that unite stronger elements.

HORIZONTALLY SPEAKING

The word "groundcover" is about as catchall as it comes. What plant, from some perspective, doesn't cover ground? On horizontal planes, some structural plants ramble along like herbaceous groundcovers, smartly cloaking visible soil left naked by larger plants. They fill the voids, tie things together, and even offer an alternative to lawns, whether by choice or virtue of context.

Euonymus fortunei 'Wolong Ghost'.

The name *Euonymus* conjures up mixed feelings in people—sometimes disdain and sometimes elation. Sure, I get tired of seeing crappy, variegated, scale-infested selections of *E. fortunei* climb up the foundation of my local shopping mall, but those poor schmucks are hardly representative of a genus, much less a species, otherwise full of plants with fine foliage and occasionally astounding fruits. One of its selections, which I've enjoyed for years in my garden, is 'Wolong Ghost', brought into cultivation by intrepid plant explorer Dan Hinkley of the former Heronswood Nursery. Discovered in the Wolong Nature Preserve, this handsome form owes its ornamental virtues to narrow, jade green leaves bisected by a sharp, white midrib—in a word, electric. I first grew this back in the early 2000s, planting it in the shade of an old weigela that eventually outgrew its circumstance. Despite the shade, 'Wolong Ghost' persisted underneath, all the while shiny, lustrous, and calling for attention. It's increasingly abundant in commerce, tremendously adaptable (so long as it grows in well-drained soil), and relatively hardy through zone 5, though I do notice a little tip dieback in especially hard winters. More people should grow this.

Despite its incredible diversity (its 750 species include everything from woody groundcovers to shrubs and small trees), the genus *Indigofera* isn't well known in horticulture. *Indigofera kirilowii* (Chinese

indigo) is a zone-5-hardy woody groundcover that fills voids in a way few other plants can, bridging gaps from full sun to full shade. It flowers in late spring and early summer at only twelve to fourteen inches tall, its strings of pink, wisteria-like flowers glistening and dangling against a backdrop of typically pinnate, pendent leaflets that owe much to their legume heritage. It's not rampant, spreading modestly by stolons, and I wish it was a smidge more vigorous. As an aside and on the more sizable end of the indigo spectrum, *I. amblyantha* expands on everything that's wonderful about its diminutive cousin. A shrub from four to eight feet high and wide, it flowers profusely for months on the current season's growth, gracing gardens in zone 5b and higher with spires of rose-colored peas. Once established, it's drought tolerant and a staple of the progressive mixed border.

For covering ground in shade, the world of irises offers many options, most notably the crested irises. The North American native crested iris (*Iris cristata*) and Japanese roof iris (*I. tectorum*), cousins from different continents, are easy to grow, forgiving, and readily divisible: one gardener can easily start a neighborhood trend. Few flowers look so intended for the floor, and these carpet woodland gardens in blue and purple hues and occasionally white. A late spring visit to the American Horticultural Society's River Farm in Alexandria, Virginia, rekindled my joy for 'Alba', the white form of *I. tectorum*. It is abundant on the property there, a snowy butterfly of a flower that hovers over low mounds of horizontally inclined foliage and rhizomes. Lacy and delicate, a clump in the shade garden often looks too perfect to be real. *Iris tectorum* thrives in dry soil, while *I. cristata* prefers more consistently moist soils, though on balance both are remarkably adaptable. These dainty irises are the perfect harmonizers to epimediums.

Like many groundcovers, dwarf Solomon's seal (*Polygonatum humile*) is one of those little details left for playful intermissions between louder, sassier groupings of plants. Ever running around the garden floor in search of a neighbor, dwarf Solomon's seal never grows more than six or eight inches tall. Little fluted stems with white, teardrop-shaped flowers fall open early in spring and join an ephemeral crowd at full tilt—violets, hepaticas, and *Mitella* to name a few.

Similar in disposition, yellow fairy bells (*Disporum flavens*) lights up quiet, dull corners of the shade garden, one small troupe at a time. The Asian native forms humble colonies that ultimately reach thirty inches tall in a growing season, though flowering often commences around a foot into the ascent. What more needs to be said about plants that are so easy to grow? Drop the roots into some decent humus, cool in the shade, and you're on your way to enjoying these little votives of the woodland garden.

Sticking to yellow, *Aquilegia canadensis* 'Corbett' comes to mind as a tamer alternative to the weedier eastern columbines. Long championed

Korean dwarf goatsbeard (*Aruncus aethusifolius*).

(left) *Aquilegia canadensis* 'Corbett'.

by Allan Armitage, this yellow dwarf came to American horticulture thanks to the eagle eyes of two Boy Scouts from Corbett, Maryland. In full flower the plant and all its profuse pendants rivals the finest lumieres for intensity and brightness. Plant for close encounters at the edge of paths or bed lines.

DOWN LOW

Mind you, I've never been particularly fond of *Aruncus*, mainly because standard forms of *A. dioicus* in full bloom look like bleached blondes after a bad rock concert, not to mention their ogreish proportions. If that's your style, find a dimly lit corner of the garden where nothing else will grow and give it a shot. Contrastingly, in the common name department, *Aruncus* comes close to evoking the quality of a nice goatee (goatsbeard), which earns it double points, because really, what guy doesn't dream of sporting a sexy goatee, if even for a minute?

But there's more to life with *Aruncus* than bleached blondes after a bad rock concert—a few selections keep it on the DL. Under the pretty and petite sign that you won't find at your local garden center, you'll encounter Korean dwarf goatsbeard (*A. aethusifolius*), which offers a supremely charming lesson in what a little manipulation of scale does for the garden's design. At first sight the flowers, which virtually engulf the plants in full bloom, more closely resemble an astilbe than the stringy flowers of its taller cousin. They're prim and proper, stately and classy, and in a twelve- to fourteen-inch mound, they effuse an

In dramatic flower, *Epimedium* 'Sunshowers' brightens the darkest corners of the shade garden.

irresistibly old-school charm. Planted in clusters at the front of the border, dotted along its length, you might as well collapse on yourself in self-satisfaction. In leaf alone, there's no sugar-coating what's not there—they are kind of boring. No doubt, the foliage is *lovely*, lacily cut and dissected—it's the perfect greenery to fill out a bouquet picked on a garden walk. But the magic is in the mix, nature's brilliant combination of ascendant flowers and enviably ferny foliage. Making the rounds of nursery catalogs recently is 'Guinea Fowl' (well, that's about the size of it), an apparent hybrid between the aforementioned charmer *A. aethusifolius* and its monster cousin *A. dioicus*, from German perennial guru Ernst Pagels. Boasting a dizzying number of flowers, it might well be the new cream of the crop in a group of plants with a limited number of cultivars.

Epimediums are stalwarts of the shade garden, barberry relatives that have earned every ounce of focus and attention they've received since their star turn began circa 1990. Darrell Probst is the reigning master here, having developed dozens of hybrids that explore every color from russet and amber to strawberry and lemon. The bicolors are smashing, too. The list of notable cultivars runs long. Starting with the regulars, *Epimedium ×versicolor* 'Sulphureum' is a golden oldie. Rampant and ravishing, red-mottled leaves form dense stands—the ultimate groundcover, particularly in dry soils. In full flower it's head-turning, with masses of bitone, spidery flowers clouding the air. On a similar theme, the aptly named 'Sunshowers' shoots shreds of the celestial

An almost garish combination for spring gardens: prairie ragwort (*Packera plattensis*) consorting with *Salvia nemorosa*.

Hylomecon japonicum.

Giant deadnettle (*Lamium orvala*).

Saruma henryi.

orb across the garden floor in a springtime show that makes me giddy. 'Amber Queen', a newer hybrid from the United Kingdom, is among the best available. With orange-tipped flowers dripping with jesterly charm, it will bewitch your checkbook. Each cluster of a bazillion flowers emanates from an arching two-foot flower stalk that nods over neighboring plants, seeming to dote upon them.

Hylomecon japonicum is a fabulous little woodland poppy from Japan that slowly forms a billowing mound of golden, four-petaled flowers in late spring. Once you have a clump big enough to divide, you won't want to share. As a mature, established mass, it's a sight to behold. While slow to take off, once firmly rooted after a few seasons, the plants grow and reward in well-mannered abundance.

Packera plattensis, known in common parlance as prairie ragwort, is anything but raggy or worty. By all accounts it's a common weed, though among the showiest. It reseeds like philanthropists give money, but remember the rules of environment—in a garden built on ecological goodness, a community finds ways to balance its members. If you need to weed it out, do so and reduce the population available to set seed. In the meantime, it will knit together the patchwork garden with golden flowers and plenty of puffy white seeds. Planted alongside salvias, emanating from within mats of ajuga, or disrupting heavenly hosts of epimediums, it's a dandy companion plant.

Okay, so call me addicted to yellow in the shade. In a part of the garden so easily dampened with cool blues and alluring greens, it never hurts to invest in plants that challenge the status quo. Of all these geeky treasures vying for popularity, *Saruma henryi* tops the list. The genus name is an anagram of its nearest relative—*Asarum*—the wild gingers of greater fame. *Saruma henryi* won't stop traffic—its flowers are hardly brazen but rather small, round, and buttery, alighting atop fuzzy, heart-shaped leaves. But not every plant has to stop traffic. Plants with softer personalities add depth to garden vignettes, an idea worth exploring in another chapter.

On the subject of depth, giant deadnettle (*Lamium orvala*) caught my attention several years ago as a lamium of distinction. Unlike the silvery slithering forms commonly available (I have no prejudice here, mind you, just an earnest interest in something different), this plant doesn't so much cover ground as it fills voids. Rotund in shape, it's a stockier version of familiar deadnettles, lumbering upward to nearly three feet in height—the puffy pillow amid a sea of blankets. This species blooms for a shorter period of spring and early summer than its cousins but does so profusely—dense clusters of pink flowers line the terminus of each square stem.

There are meadow rues, too, that hover near the ground, offering all the beauty of their airborne relatives, only on a smaller scale. Chief among these starry carpets is the delicate *Thalictrum kiusianum*, a

Thalictrum ichangense 'Evening Star'.

(opposite) *Thalictrum minus* 'Adiantifolium'.

groundcovering species with flowers as miniature as its leaves. Clouds of pinkish flowers float above classic, blue-green foliage that never seems to melt or succumb to the onslaught of summer—the ideal plant for the part shade rock garden or bordering the garden path. Once you've cooed over *T. kiusianum*, you might consider upgrading to the equally cute *T. ichangense* 'Evening Star', a dazzling, silver-dappled selection with coin-sized leaves. The best part? It knows no flowering season, powering from spring through fall in a regular succession of eight-inch-tall sprays of frothy light lavender flowers. In my own garden, it's survived seasonal droughts and zone-4 winters and still has nothing but charms to extol.

Thalictrum minus 'Adiantifolium' is another of the highly cute, daintily proportioned meadow rues that no garden should be without. In my garden, I have it planted within the border, staged to view through and against its companions—a curious cloud of green flowers flickering above foliage reminiscent of maidenhair ferns (*Adiantum*). Don't let its meek aesthetic fool you—it's a tough plant, bone-hardy to zone 3 and happy to go dormant in dry times to weather through for another spring appeal.

EMBLEMS

KEEPING PACE WITH THE SEASONS

Things have their period; even excellences
are subject to fashion.

—Balthasar Gracian,
The Art of Worldly Wisdom (1647)

Each season has its emblem plants, timepiece essentials that bring
gardeners joy. Emblems are often familiar things, a dose of old favorites
in contrast to an expanding horticultural vocabulary. After all, emblems
define our expectations for each passing season; without them, the garden might smear into a blur, May mumbling into August and September
senescing into March. Think of May and all its irises and lilacs and
peonies. In July Oriental lilies take their cue. Come September it's colchicums and chrysanthemums. Turn, turn, turn. Part of chasing after
the modern, eclectic garden is minding the importance of plants that
only do it once, the one-hit, offbeat wonders of the garden's seasonal
cadence. We should revel in that cadence, amid the steadfast presence
of plants that endure the seasonal shifts with constancy and resilience.
Planting emblems celebrates diversity in the seasons in which it shines,
and in every season, there are definitively emblematic plants.

Winter aconite (*Eranthis hyemalis*) is a beloved emblem of late winter and early spring, here naturalized by the tens of thousands at Fernwood Botanical Garden, Niles, Michigan.

(opposite) Even non-gardeners could probably pick a Shasta daisy out of a lineup. But as familiar as this stalwart summer flowerer is, new varieties like this *Leucanthemum ×superbum* 'Victorian Secret' redefine it for a new generation of gardeners, offering even better vigor, tidy habit, and ruffled blooms.

WINTER

Let's start where the calendar starts, in winter. The winter garden was romanticized by the great garden writers of old—so many of whom gardened in the United Kingdom or milder, temperate climates where winters were worth romanticizing. For most gardeners in northern temperate climates, winter may be politely described as a period of rest and reflection. Leaving politeness aside? Winter—too often—sucks. Yet in the Southeast and the Pacific Northwest in particular, the winter garden is a treasure box of jewels prized for their resilience in an otherwise bleak season. In northern climates, by comparison, the winter garden is really the early spring garden, a brief window of perhaps three weeks where temperatures gather the strength to finally break winter's iron fist. No matter the geography, positioning your garden so that it can take advantage of these rare first moments of amiable weather comes down to imaginative and resourceful plant selection.

SHRUBS THAT DO IT FIRST

There's something to be said about being first. As the snow melts, the floral whispers of late winter prequel the roaring rush of June and July. These first, hushed moments in the garden are provided by a trio of winter-flowering shrubs, whose genetic programming insistently cues their flowers amid frigid temperatures.

The first of the three genera, *Edgeworthia*, has long incited my zonal denial. Fuzzy and fetching cauliflower buds unfurl into trumpets that sound golden, red, and even orange notes of the coming spring. Edgeworthias have a storied history in Eastern culture as the source of pulp used in the production of fine stationery and bank notes (hence the common name, paperbush). The annual performance, a horticultural striptease of sorts, typically opens in November or December, when the parasol frame sheds its leaves, revealing powdery smooth, gray-brown bark and ensuring an unobstructed view of the floral presentation, which begins as early as February and continues through March and April. As daytime temperatures rise, rich, heady aromas emanate from open blossoms. After the flowers, the leathery gray-green leaves return for the summer—an exceptional textural note to whatever vignette they join. Several selections exist, all choice and rarefied variations on a desirable theme. Tony Avent's 'Snow Cream', sold through Plant Delights Nursery, is characterized by vigorous growth, large flowers, and an arborescent proportion at maturity, commonly eight to twelve feet high. In 'Akebono', each devilishly handsome red flower is carried in clusters smaller than those of the species. I've yet to meet a form I didn't like: all my powers of discernment are overwhelmed by my envy of gardeners who can cultivate these plants.

In Oregon, *Edgeworthia chrysantha* sheds its leaves to poetic effect in early November, here at the Portland Japanese Garden.

The flowers of *Edgeworthia chrysantha* reward close inspection.

(right) *Hamamelis vernalis* 'Amethyst' in flower at Don Shadow's farm near Winchester, Tennessee.

In much of the North, you'll be hard-pressed to find anything in bloom on 15 March (beware the ides of March!). You'd be lucky to find hellebores unfurling in sheltered southern exposures, or perhaps some snowdrops poking above the mulch. So I've always been fond of vernal witchhazel (*Hamamelis vernalis*), the first woody plant to flower across much of the region, often blooming through cold snaps and snows, abiding by its evolutionary programming to give the finger to whatever weather comes its way. Vernal witchhazel is native to the Ozarks of southern Missouri and northern Arkansas, a relict of the last glacial advance, which left a number of species stranded atop a rising plateau. Its flowers are small and many and spicy to the sniff. 'Amethyst', discovered by Ohio nurseryman Tim Brotzman, is coveted for its purple flowers, a splendid alternative to the species' usual rusty browns and golds—though in such early days, any color is welcome.

Most witchhazel cultivars on the market owe their ancestry to two Asian species—*Hamamelis japonica* (Japanese witchhazel) and *H. mollis* (Chinese witchhazel). These *H.* ×*intermedia* hybrids, hardy to zone 5, grow into large shrubs and small trees topping out at anywhere from eight to fifteen feet tall and wide and occasionally bigger still. In season, they rule the winter garden with beguiling flowers. In summer, they blend into the background, rough-hewn and muscular in structure.

In fall, they give a foliar encore, burning through the closing weeks of autumn with fiery tenacity. 'Arnold Promise' is a classic among classics. 'Magic Fire' is lacquered in alluring redness. 'Jelena', a European selection, gives orange zest a run for its money. 'Treasure Trove' induced drooling when I first encountered it, a feast for winter-weary eyes with bright frilly clusters of yellow flowers almost two inches across.

Hamamelis virginiana, our eastern North American native witchhazel, is the exception to the generic winter-flowering rule. It blooms in autumn—it had to be different—often through Thanksgiving, flanked in yellow flannel leaves, to the bewilderment of most gardeners. You could say it just gets a head start on the rest of the bunch, opening the door that its vernal relatives close. Regardless, in a plant-driven landscape, no small token of floral charm is taken for granted, particularly in late autumn.

Finally—in the category of looks like a witchhazel, but isn't—winterhazels (*Corylopsis*) are equally bewitching. A mature shrub dazzles, loaded with hundreds of yellow wind chimes, layered one on top of the other up and down the length of ascendant stems. In late winter, viewed from a distance, it looks sculptural and self-lit, perfect for drawing the

Hamamelis ×intermedia 'Treasure Trove' is a vigorous variety with a broad, horizontal habit selected by famed horticulturists Jelena and Robert de Belder of Belgium.

Corylopsis spicata glowing from a distance.

eye through the landscape, past the browns of dormancy to the glimmers of early spring. The eventual leaves are interesting, too, ribbed and ridged in green, as fine as a pair of pleated pants that nobody wears anymore. Fall comes, and the shrub dons yellow again, this time in a leafy cloak that lasts for weeks. Emblematic in two seasons, a well-placed winterhazel is hard to best.

HELLA WONDERFUL

Back in the last century, hellebores were a local garage band with a loyal but modest following, hammering out a new sound. Now, they are rock stars, selling out engagements countrywide. Hybrids abound—somewhere between their free-seeding nature and deft hybridizing, a race of incredible garden plants has taken hellebores to new heights. Amazing books on the subject have already appeared, in particular Cole Burrell's and Judith Tyler's well-photographed and thoroughly researched monograph, *Hellebores*, so I feel inept at offering even meager appraisals. Many, though, would agree that Marietta and Ernie O'Byrne of Eugene, Oregon, have mastered the double-flowered realm of the genus. The names under which they are sold make them seem destined for

Helleborus foetidus 'Red Silver', a seed strain, plays up its green-belled flowers with daggered leaves, red-hued and shot with shades of pewter throughout.

(top) *Helleborus ×ericsmithii* 'Winter Sunshine'.

(opposite top) The double-flowered *Helleborus* 'Jade Tiger' (Winter Jewels).

(opposite bottom) *Helleborus* 'Anna's Red'.

immortality—'Onyx Odyssey', 'Golden Lotus', 'Jade Tiger'. But the list of people involved with hellebore breeding runs long—anyone who gardens with more than a few hellebores eventually ends up with a strain of their own. Judith and Dick Tyler are among the best at breeding and selecting; their strong plants are sold in series bearing their Pine Knot Farms moniker. David Culp of Brandywine Cottage in Pennsylvania offers seedlings selected from his hillside gardens as the Brandywine Strain, the best-known of which are intense satin blacks. Barry Glick of Sunshine Farm and Gardens has pollinated double and single flowers on full plants which he markets as Sunshine Selections.

Helleborus 'Anna's Red' is a new powerhouse from the United Kingdom, boasting red-pink flowers that bowl over even the staunchest hellebore skeptics. The color is enviable, the marbled foliage maybe more so. And *H. ×ericsmithii* hybrids, those owing ancestry to *H. niger* and *H. ×sternii*, not only offer large, outfacing flowers in rosy blends of green, cream, and white but rigid, plastic foliage that lasts through the growing season. Anyone who grows hellebores should continue to critically judge the foliage after the flowers fade—anything that holds up, stays taut and crisp, deserves admiration. I've watched too many of the worst of them cave under the pressure of summer. A gardener should be able to admire the emblem but enjoy the offseason.

Along with drought-tolerance, broad adaptability to most gardens zones 4 through 9, and unpalatability to deer, species like *Helleborus foetidus* (stinking hellebore), *H. purpurascens* (purple winter rose), and *H. argutifolius* (Corsican hellebore) reliably find their way into gardens for their elegant textures and flowers. By commercial standards, in their unrefined condition, these species are mere precursors to the elaborations of plant breeders, but to anyone fond of something curious, they are covetable. Selections of the species, of which there are many, make equally impressive additions to gardens. Here I must mention the Helleborus Gold Collection, a series of vegetatively propagated *H. niger* (Christmas rose) selections, mostly in shades of white with plastic foliage; the earliest of hellebores to bloom (the common name should give a clue), these holiday spectacles actually make great houseplants. Held over for spring planting, they fill out into robust garden clumps with emerald green foliage. 'Jacob' was my initial introduction to the series, but he's been bested with 'Jacob Classic' and 'Jacob Royal'. 'Josef Lemper' is worth a try, too.

SPRING

Spring is full of cheap, satisfying thrills. It's easy to make pretty in spring, drunk on the poetry of silver rains, flowers everywhere, and poetry itself—in this season, the world is indeed what Cummings called it, mud-luscious and puddle-wonderful. And perhaps because of all this, spring is also full of emblems that endure in American gardens. But spring is tyrannous—its effusion hogs the first third of the growing season on garden center shelves, resulting in a bias toward May and June and an indifference to the rest of the calendar. But there's no need for bitterness. Embracing all the seasons and their diversity just means growing more plants, which is what the world needs more of anyway.

One of the anticipated spring ephemerals in my garden is spring pea (*Lathyrus vernus*). The genus *Lathyrus* is quite diverse and best known for its vines—the sweet peas of our grandmothers' back fences. But the spring pea doesn't mount, it mounds, growing into a comely clump that overflows with scapes of pink and lavender flowers in part shade. In general, these vernal peas are too rare in the garden and for no good reason. Early spring flowering, delicate, and tough as nails—what more could you want?

Common snowdrop (*Galanthus nivalis*).

DROPS, DRIBLETS, SPOTS, AND SPECKS

These nouns not only capture the pace at which spring so often begins but the personalities of the plants it keeps. Ephemerals are the alpha emblems of the season, even if their personalities as plants wouldn't suggest it. They are programmed to sprout, flower, and set seed within a very small window—get up, put out, and get back to bed. For the moments they last, they are joyous, the first flowers to color the landscape.

Snowdrops (*Galanthus*) are among the earliest hints of spring, verdant notes from a dormant score. Snowdrops are also definite characters, even if their detractors deride them for being merely green and white (and occasionally yellow). Distinguished horticulturist Gertrude Wister made the point in writing years ago: "The flowers of late winter and early spring occupy places in our hearts well out of proportion to their size." Though diminutive and limited in color, snowdrops are a fleeting sensation for which enthusiasm flows in the absence of other flowers. Even the common snowdrop (*G. nivalis*), which you can cheaply buy dozens of, deserves to be planted abundantly.

Bona fide galanthophiles—plant geeks of a clinical ilk—could list dozens of essential varieties for those who want to dive off the deep end. Among those classics, *Galanthus elwesii* var. *monostictus* offers some of the largest flowers, each characterized by a single large green mark

on the inner tepals. The Hiemalis Group, a selection of the latter, turns heads for its bloom time—late fall, usually around Thanksgiving or even Christmas. *Galanthus plicatus* and its cultivars are the standard-setting snowdrops, shapely and voluminously flowered, against which all others are compared. Forms flower from Christmas ('Three Ships') well into March ('Washfield Warham'), extending their spectacle to the joy of now-converted enthusiasts. Remember, in the world of snowdrops, there really is no joking about growing only the green and white ones.

In March, in the woodlands I tramped through on warm afternoons in college, hepaticas flowered by the thousands. Carpeting the forest floor with bands of blue and sashes of white, these tiny, five-petaled flowers enchanted my senses, much as galanthus do now. After a long winter, I'll tip my hat to any spot of color brave enough to push through a crust of last autumn's fallen leaves. Hepaticas enchant even before they flower, their three-lobed, silver-splattered leaves, purpled by weeks of freezing temperatures, glowing against the ground. With little else to be fascinated by, this will do.

Along with hepaticas in those woods grew snow trillium (*Trillium nivale*), a white spark from a genus replete with springtime emblems. Even at the smallest end of the scale, it's an essential definer of a season just beginning. Planted in tufts, the mass lasts for a few days. Yes, there's nothing long-lasting about these ephemerals: they are the ultimate botanical wham-bam, but I guess the alternative—nothing-ness—isn't terribly exciting, either. Trilliums in general seem to define a certain maturation of a gardener's finer tastes—the pearls of elder sensibility. Though not difficult to grow, the prices at which they sell weed out the risk-averse. Not all are out of reach, and for any gardener willing to invest, the rewards are great. Take bloody butcher (*T. recurvatum*), for example, and not just because it has a common name worth repeating. Teasing sanguine with simple claws, the flowers sit flush against an elegant platter of draping leaves. In woodsy soils with plenty of organic matter, you'll have no problem growing a fine clump to the envy of gardening friends. Of course the prototypical trillium is *T. grandiflorum*, the amply flowered perennial that colonizes and spreads across the woodland garden and at least half of Michigan.

In the white and early spring department, bloodroot (*Sanguinaria canadensis*) is ever in style. My first ritualistic encounters with blood-root were in the ten acres of oak savanna on my family farm. Each spring, I would sojourn into the woods, scouring the ground floor for crowds of my favorite ephemerals—*Claytonia*, *Erythronium*, *Cardamine*, and bloodroot. Named for the morphine-like substance exuded from their rhizomes, which I had to discover for myself as a youth, bloodroot makes an easy groundcover in the woodland garden, slowly spreading over the years to form a carpet of pristine, virginal flowers that harbinger spring.

The double 'Multiplex' trumps any of the rest—a mark of fine taste. A loosely defined cultivar (no doubt any double mutation discovered over time has donned this name), it's finally more available, descending from its lofty three-figure price tag into an affordable range. Collectors have long cosseted their clumps of 'Multiplex', hoarding them behind tall trees in the farthest reaches of the shade garden for fear of them being stolen (which has happened—smart crooks). Though it clumps at a moderate pace, it's hardly so slow as to warrant obscurity. Hailed by the Royal Horticultural Society as one of the top plant introductions of the last two hundred years, it's a dashing, double-petaled example of our native North American flora and the impact such gems have had on international horticulture.

I'm not ashamed to admit that I have a lusty affair with *Corydalis*. As free advice goes, more gardeners should. Every garden has weeds, so why not plant a few of them yourself? Even novice gardeners can grow amiable profusions of *C. solida*, the appleblossom-shaded species that reseeds freely in soils with even nominal fertility. Over the years I've encouraged its free spirit, assisting its romp through the gardenhood by throwing its dehiscent seed pods into various corners where I could do with a spot of color. Plants break into colorful swathes in early spring, shortly after the rush of *Galanthus*; I couldn't imagine the pace of spring without them. Once you get your feet wet with *C. solida*, you can easily upgrade your fascination to *C. nobilis*. Linnaeus was only the first of many to be extremely fond of this plant (as his epithet for it, "the noble one," suggests); indeed, this queen of the genus earns my loyalty every spring with bevies of golden flowers tipped with a little black spot, a beauty mark befitting this prettiest of faces. It's not only queen of the genus, but queen of the shade garden when in flower, delivering a shocking jolt of color when everything else wants to play in pastel. After several seasons of trying to successfully grow plants from seed, I finally raised a few to flowering size, and I've been blessed ever since. If you're trying to procure a few of your own, seek out a good nursery and let them suffer through low germination and seedling die-off on your behalf. Once planted, nature does the rest.

(clockwise from top)
Corydalis solida.

Fern-leafed corydalis (*Corydalis cheilanthifolia*), hardy to zone 6, flares from the crevices of this rock wall at Philadelphia's Morris Arboretum in late March.

Corydalis nobilis, once established, is prone to well-mannered reseeding.

(clockwise from top left)
Flame tulip (*Tulipa acuminata*).

Tulipa clusiana 'Cynthia' chiming in with the rusty browns of last season's little bluestem (*Schizachyrium scoparium*).

Tulipa vvedenskyi.

Tulipa linifolia 'Apricot Jewel'.

TULIP MANIA

Mention spring in conversation and tulips can't be far from mind. They are chief contributors to vernal tyranny, even if we love them just the same. While bulbous and perennial by definition, most varieties that we find in bulk bins at the garden center in fall are truly intended for annual consumption, even if beguiling photos of luscious flowers with Dutch blue skies suggest otherwise. There's nothing as Dutch as the Netherlands itself. The rest of us have to swallow reality with a hard gulp.

But not all tulips are created equal. In fact, the roster of truly perennial tulips is a list of red-shirted benchwarmers relegated to the gardens of the few instead of the many. For shame. Take the flame tulip (*Tulipa acuminata*), for example, the Lady Gaga of tulips, native to meadows in Turkey. Its twisted-petaled flowers scream for attention in mid-May. They always look photogenic and are irresistible planted in drifts.

If you have the inclination, building a rock garden or at the very least a bed with a little more gravel in it will open up Pandora's Box of assorted tulips. At least three border on essential in these circumstances—*Tulipa vvedenskyi*, a Russian tulip if you hadn't guessed from the name; *T. clusiana* and its cultivars 'Cynthia' and 'Lady Jane'; and *T. linifolia*. *Tulipa vvedenskyi* has delightfully corrugated leaves with profound ripples that would hold interest even if the fiery red flowers never showed up. Up and down the Front Range, gardeners have deftly installed these in hellstrips and front yards as an example to the rest of us. More adaptable than its provenance or present cultivated range would suggest, this Russian tulip of montane meadows is short and not for cutting—plant nearest a path or close to the front door for constant enjoyment.

In contrast, *Tulipa clusiana* makes a fine cut flower, its wiry, supple stems terminating in flowers of demure size but robust colors. 'Cynthia' grows in my front yard scree garden, joining the remnant stems of little bluestem that I annually leave to stand the winter snows, partly out of laziness (or lack of priorities) and partly just to create this vignette. She is a pleasant reminder of my alma mater (my undergraduate adviser shares the name), flowers banded and flushed cardinal and gold.

Last in the triptych, though certainly not least—*Tulipa linifolia* (sometimes still sold as *T. batalinii*). This Soviet-region species grows in scree environments in the wild, a useful indicator of where best to use it in the landscape—rock gardens, troughs, and even hellstrips. Often entirely yellow or red in the wild, a number of color forms exist, including 'Apricot Jewel' with its gemstone-perfect, three-sided orbs that glow in peachy tones. Touched with a hint of rose at the base, the flowers rise from a rosette of sea green foliage, ever so lightly crinkled at the margins, unraveling the spring.

INDULGING NARCISSISM

In the horticultural context, narcissism—otherwise known as planting daffodils with unfettered abandon—is practically requisite. With their passion for the subject, my friends Brent and Becky Heath have certainly encouraged this in me and many thousands of other gardeners by distributing fine hybrids for decades. Daffodils are timeless, overall rodent-proof, and come in enough colors and shapes to satisfy any taste or whim, as the thirteen descriptive divisions of the American Daffodil Society attest. Hands down, they are the easiest perennials to make gardens with; their unfailing annual flowering in ditches, cemeteries, and historic sites is testament to their durability and persistence. 'Hillstar' (Division 7) has grown in my garden since I was ten years old. I bought the bulbs at a big box store, no doubt with allowance money I'd hoarded for the explicit purpose of splurging on same. And they've thrived in the same spot since, lurking in dormancy beneath the full crowns of established hostas and bleeding hearts. Nothing else in my garden has given me so much pleasure for so little effort. That clump of 'Hillstar' blooms generously every year, its yellow-sparked white flowers the starshine of the woodland garden in mid-spring. The bottom line is simple—plant daffodils, lots of them, and reap joy. For anyone similarly enthralled with throngs of buttery flowers, whole books extol the many charms, particulars, and exacting definitions of the genus.

'Rijvnveld's Early Sensation' (Division 1) is a garden standard, the earliest flowering of the trumpet daffodils. In the South, it's no stretch to see it bloom in February, snow-capped flowers carried on foot-tall stems. Hellebores welcome its colorful companionship, as do the crocuses (if it hasn't already beaten them to the punch). This variety naturalizes effortlessly and persists in the same spot for (almost) ever, to the delight of winter-weary gardeners everywhere.

Loving modern art as I do, I'm biased. But 'Modern Art' (Division 2), the daffodil, stands on its own merits with a pertly ruffled orange cup staged against bright yellow. Planted in drifts, this 1973 introduction looks devilish in companion with *Fritillaria persica*—bold strokes of black, yellow, and orange for a robust urban color scheme.

'Rip Van Winkle' (Division 4) is a silly little thing, never quite knowing if it's a spidery mess of green petals or a miniature, double daffodil. No matter its personality, sometimes split among stems in the same clump, I love it. Tiny leaves and quirky, twinkling flowers grace the ground early in spring, often just as the dwarf *Iris pumila* begins to flower (smashing combination of purple and yellow, by the way). Grow leanly and plant lots at the outset (they are cheap). They persist and, if happy enough, will naturalize in time.

I eagerly await the return of 'Rapture' (Division 6) each spring as its nodding, poetic flowers sinuously thread yellow in and through the accumulated debris of the winter garden. Like golden cigars, these

tubular flowers light up the understory of my front yard, needing no companion to make pretty. So easy, I needn't even mention cultural information.

'Blushing Lady' (Division 7) flowers in Easter colors: rich pastel pink cups backlit by lemon meringue. With up to five buds per stem, this classic jonquil-type daffodil sports pleasantly scented flowers that combine nicely with *Anemone coronaria* (if you're into blousy, crepe-papery flowers) or *Fritillaria pallidiflora* (if you're a bulb geek).

'Mary Gay Lirette' (Division 11) is a good example of the split-cup daffodils I so adore for their freakish profusion of un-daffodil-like petals. The Heaths named this for a local musician in their community, who I imagine was a beautiful, talented woman to have such a fine daffodil named for her. Its lacy, cheery-colored blooms prevent the mud from sullying my optimism for spring. Early in that season, these yellow-cupped daffodils fade to a harmonious array of salmon against white, each at its own pace, making for a multitude of shifting colors. I wouldn't garden without it.

'W. P. Milner' (Division 13), cultivated since the middle of the 19th century, is a classic harbinger of spring that not enough people know. This charming heirloom flowers at only six inches tall, its twisty white and cream petals nodding in the face of freezing rain or snowy fits. It looks smart in containers, the perfect miniature daff for a spring-themed pot on the balcony or deck.

Corn leaf iris (*Iris bucharica*).

AN IRIS FOR EVERY GARDEN

What's an iris lover supposed to say when asked about his favorite emblem of spring? I'll try not to gush. Of course I believe every garden should have irises. Why not? Beyond the bearded irises, of which there are thousands you must grow, there's really an iris for almost every circumstance and opportunity. Irises truly offer a parade of diversity that begins in early spring and continues strong through summer.

With a name like corn leaf iris, *Iris bucharica*, one of the true bulbous irises, deserves a spot in every corn-belt garden in company with something blue to make those aureolin yellow flowers zing. Amid the spring awakening, corn leaf irises are as essential as salt and pepper. Easy, drought tolerant, and a quick colonizer.

'Dazzling' is an astoundingly beautiful intermediate bearded iris bred by my friend Paul Black of Salem, Oregon. It's a reliable performer everywhere from California to Iowa to Maine, charming the eye with sea blue falls below snow white standards. For the modern garden short on space, this clump queen is essential.

If I said Siberian irises, you might reply with 'Caesar's Brother' or 'Butter and Sugar', two good answers, but neither A-plus in grade. In fact, there *is* more to Siberian irises than the blues and yellows of old would suggest. 'Ginger Twist' sounds like my kind of cocktail, a fact I'm reminded of each time I see a dazzling clump of this Siberian iris. What

Iris 'Dazzling'.

(right) *Iris* 'Ginger Twist'.

Iris 'Pomegranate Punch'.

(left) Iris laevigata 'Lakeside Ghost'.

Iris spuria ssp. *halophila* 'Prairie Lights'.

a show it puts on, flowers fizzing in ginger, amber, and golden tones. 'Pomegranate Punch' certainly headlines the party menu. If you've only laid eyes on the usual suspects, you might think Siberians were boring until you drank in these luscious, fruity flowers. With plenty of buds and good vigor, this new-age Siberian leads the pack in the early summer garden and is a solid performer in many climates. Who wouldn't want the newest in Siberians with a nod to mixology?

Iris laevigata 'Lakeside Ghost' is a fantastic representative of perhaps the most classic of water irises. Long popular in the United Kingdom, the Japanese *I. laevigata* is strangely absent from American gardens. Plants thrive in shallow water, so they are perfect for the margins of ponds or even bog gardens. Like the classic *I. ensata* and other Japanese irises, they do best in slightly acidic soils (pH 5.5 to 6.0), which results in crisp green blades that give rise to saucer-sized flowers in shades of blue, purple, and white. 'Lakeside Ghost' is a newer selection from Chad Harris at Mt. Pleasant Iris Farm in Washington, an eerily pale selection with finely splattered blue markings.

In a final nod to emblematic irises of my own late spring garden: let's hear it for spuria irises. Too few gardeners appreciate them, and they remain barely recognizable to even the most astute plant collectors. Passed along for decades, *Iris orientalis* (syn. *I. ochroleuca*) is about as far into the section as most gardeners get, and it's no shrinking violet of a plant, mind you. Bordering on brutish, it's big, pearly in blossom, and takes whatever you dish it. A well-established clump can flower for weeks in midsummer, the perfect digestif after the blowsiness of spring irises. But there's a whole world of exceptional colors in this section worth relishing. Those few hybridizers who have taken up the spuria cause have left formative impressions: bronzes, golds, rusts, oranges, and bicolors have joined the usual array of blue, purple, orchid, and white, making for striking flowers, elegantly constructed and prime for cutting. 'Prairie Lights', a recent selection of mine, is a hardworking and early flowering clone of *I. spuria* ssp. *halophila* that overlaps in flower with tall bearded irises; its pale yellow and white flowers hover over the clump, a treat for flower-conscious gardeners.

Paeonia 'Cheese Country'.

PEONIES, PLEASE

Again with the gaudy classics. 'Coral Charm' charms me every spring
with tightly formed semi-double cups in jovial shades of amber and
pink that verge on indecently vibrant compared to the whitewashed
Lactiflora peonies of childhood memory. While old news in peony
circles (it's a 1978 Roy Klehm introduction), a fully blossomed clump
of 'Coral Charm' is a spectacular emblem that more gardeners should
plant. 'Cheese Country', too, shows what's colorfully possible in the
world of peonies. Pink guard petals subtend an explosion of cheddary
petaloids that terminate in a tuft of rose. If you got it, flaunt it.

Peonies have more to offer than most of us realize as new cultivars
redefine the continuum of colors associated with them. But all that's
newsworthy in peonies isn't due to flowers alone. The habits of the
older Lactiflora varieties left much to be desired, with stems genuflect-
ing and flailing to the ground not long after the last petals were shed.
No modern garden has room for such stunts. Peony expert Roy Klehm
has proffered the term "rock garden peony" to define a range of hybrids,
most owing some ancestry to the famous fernleaf peony (*Paeonia
tenuifolia*), which have exceptional compact habits, delicate foliage,
and single flowers in bright reds and pinks. 'Merry Mayshine' and 'Fairy
Princess' are definitive, particularly in the company of a proportional

Paeonia 'Garden Treasure' is indeed treasured for its every blossom, generously bestowing more and more of them upon the garden with each passing year.

boulder, which serves an aesthetic purpose but also affords them protection from the kind of garden mishaps that might injure their stems or impede flowering.

Interspecific hybrids, like the intersectional peonies of herbaceous and tree peony heritage, also continue to make inroads into mail-order catalogs, bringing peonies to an ever-growing audience of admirers. These aren't your grandmother's peonies anymore, even if they possess all the charms and durability of those vintage varieties. Among the classics is 'Garden Treasure', an immense almost-shrub bred by Don Hollingsworth, whose peony farm was just thirty minutes away from where I grew up. A product of good Midwestern selection and an American Peony Society Gold Medal winner, 'Garden Treasure', a bright lemon semi-double, delivers on the promise of its name. Often on established plants, a dozen flowers are open at once. While the show is fleeting, it's a timepiece to anticipate and celebrate.

Phlox subulata 'Coral Eyes'.

(opposite) *Phlox paniculata*
'Peppermint Twist'.

FOXY PHLOXES

"Phlox." Besides the shared terminus, the word has no relationship to "fox" (or even "vixen"), but both comparisons are apt. Even with only the handful of species mentioned here, the genus grabs and holds the gardener's attention from early spring through early summer. Native to North America and represented in American gardens since Colonial times, phloxes are the very definition of what it means to be a perennial. *Phlox paniculata* is a classic, adored for its heady clouds of flowers, gently chastised for its intolerance of powdery mildew. Modern varieties like 'Peppermint Twist', a diva of consequence, rate best-in-class for their unending floriferousness, stouter composure, and heady fragrance. Imagine a bawdy and cloying scent that hangs in the air, dripping with the dew of nightfall, a scent otherwise unassociated with conventional decency: swimming in a vat of cotton candy. Sphinx (there goes that consonant x again) moths love it, and so do I. Other varieties do what the most garden-worthy phloxes do—fiercely resist powdery mildew. Take 'Jeana', named for its discoverer Jeana Prewitt of Nashville, Tennessee: gushing with pinky effusion, miniaturized flowers unfurl into abundant panicles that attract monarchs and other flutterbys like magnets. There is something supremely satisfying about watching a stand of 'Jeana' in full flower get ravished by pollinators.

Creeping phloxes like *Phlox subulata* have found their way into rockeries (why don't people have rockeries anymore?) alongside sidewalks and embankments for nearly two centuries. Nobody's arguing it's a staple. But it's badly in need of some upgrading, because nobody likes to see their favorite carpets of color turn brown and shaggy under the stress of summer's heat. H. Lincoln Foster, a luminary of the rock gardening world during the mid-20th century, named and distributed several smashing forms of *P. subulata*, a few of which remain classics. I've grown 'Coral Eyes' with great satisfaction for nearly a decade,

Phlox 'Forever Pink' at Chicago Botanic Garden.

watching starry white flowers eyed with a dot of bright pink spill over the limestone wall of my front yard scree garden every April. These are the plants that make gardening effortless. Plant, water, and admire. Perhaps most endearing is its avoidance of the shaggy brown condition that otherwise afflicts its cousins. 'Coral Eyes' retains green and crisp foliage, a tad prickly to weed around, through summer and into fall.

Jim Ault's three recently released varieties of shorter phloxes are not only destined for the hit list, they foreshadow a revolution. Keeping with things that creep and crawl, 'Pink Profusion', a hybrid of *Phlox subulata* and *P. stolonifera* combines the best of its parents (habit from its mother; shade-tolerance from its father) to floriferous success. In bloom for up to two months in spring, 'Pink Profusion' lives up to its name, even if it's still prone to summer dormancy, the memory of which fades the following April in swarms of its flowers. 'Purple Pinwheels' is another of Ault's releases, a charming hybrid of sand phlox (*P. bifida*), a favorite of rock gardeners for decades. 'Purple Pinwheels' is ably suited to rocky or sand soils, forming tight, six-inch-tall mounds of cleft, star-shaped petals. 'Forever Pink' might well outlast its classmates in fame and garden application. Bred from fine stock (*P. glaberrima* and *P. carolina* 'Bill Baker', both hardy southeastern natives), any perennial border should have a few waves planted mid-border to color early June days. A sterile hybrid, it wastes no energy producing seed, flowering its head

Phlox pilosa ssp. *ozarkana.*

off because it doesn't know any better. It's powdery mildew resistant, compact, and even reblooms in the autumn. Check, check, check.

In closing, I have to give a nod to *Phlox pilosa* (prairie phlox), one of the finest wildflowers of the mid-states, to the tune of no less than nine subspecies! Arguably the best are ssp. *ozarkana* and ssp. *sangamonensis*, native to the Ozarks and the Sangamon River valley in central Illinois, respectively. Regardless of provenance, the lesson is a variation on a common theme—clouds of flowers (cotton candy to neon) at heights of twelve to sixteen inches, a perfect raft of pink for the spring to early summer scene.

Coreopsis 'Cranberry Ice'.

SUMMER

The summer garden is a rhapsody, alive one moment with a one-hit wonder destined for two weeks of fame, and in another with something more seasoned and reliable. The season saunters along with fleeting form and irregular pace, a colorful and pleasureful performance. In short, summer is the garden's chance to get it right, even if the season carries its baggage—thunderstorms, humidity, and drought notwithstanding. As juicy as fresh strawberries, the blooms of honeysuckles are a pleasure of early summer, even if you can't make a pie with them. What's not to love about these roving vines, coming off strong from a late spring debut for a sold-out summer series? Another pleasure is the new race of tickseeds. *Coreopsis* 'Cranberry Ice' is one such, like its fellows logging continuous months of bloom in gardens zone 6 and above. In colder climes, many of these fail to reliably perennialize, flowering their heads off without regard for crown tissue, the buds and biomass that ensure their return post-winter. Nevertheless, their colors represent extraordinary advances that many gardeners can still enjoy. Whether honeysuckles or the Next Big Thing, the flowers pile on with each passing week—perhaps the quintessential lesson of summer: let there be flowers, effusively, please.

FIRECRACKERS

Summer is hot, at least across most of temperate North America. And while not all flowers of the season compare with the temperatures, the firecrackers and spark plugs are the emblems that emblaze our memory. Take *Penstemon*, for example—new emblems, taking the long view of history. Virtually unheard of outside of collector circles until the introduction and world domination of *P. digitalis* 'Husker Red' by University of Nebraska plant breeder Dale Lindgren, penstemons have risen to new prominence. Newer varieties continue to expound on the charms of their mother, particularly 'Dark Towers' with its big satiny leaves and 'Precious Gem', a free-flowering selection in pinker shades. The genus is full of dynamite flowers in vibrant colors—firecracker reds, hot pinks (*P. barbatus*), neon blues (*P. glaber*), and even snowy whites (*P. albidus*), along with lavenders (*P. strictus*) and dozens more that I don't have space for. The firecracker penstemon of note is *P. eatonii*, whose five-alarm flowers light up xeric, intermountain gardens. High Country Gardens carries the garden-suited 'Richfield', which seduces hummingbirds each spring upon their return.

Penstemons grow with abundance in the native landscapes of the Great Plains and American Southwest, in dry to xeric conditions more often than not. Some handle water better than others; a few species like *Penstemon grandiflorus*, *P. hirsutus* (most frequent in the trade as 'Pygmaeus'), and *P. smallii* venture east to the Great Lakes and Atlantic

Penstemon richardsonii.

(left) Foxglove penstemon (Penstemon digitalis).

states, thriving famously in gardens with annual rainfall over double what they're used to farther west. Regardless of growing conditions, most species flower from a multi-stemmed crown that throws up tall stalks with pendulous vials of color. With a few exceptions, they are mid-border plants, the heavy brushstrokes that give a colorful planting its depth.

Penstemon digitalis is one of the finest wildflowers spread widely across the eastern two-thirds of the United States. When so many other penstemons try too hard to be loud—I'm thinking of the blaring, bell-flowered hybrids sold as bedding plants or tender perennials—the foxglove penstemon quietly sparkles in flower, and its seeds, held in pointy capsules, look interesting enough in December, when little else does.

Among the blues, I happened upon *Penstemon richardsonii* in an encyclopedia of Northwest native plants which had it down as occurring on snowy mountainsides in the Cascades of eastern Washington and south into Oregon. Imagine my delight when I found it thrives well beyond its dank and chilly home, as far east as the Midwest, daring to flower from low, spreading stems at the apex of summer in shades of neon blue and lavender that defy photography.

If ever there was a genus that defines (and defies) the heat of summer, *Kniphofia* does it with every raging, red-hot spike. As diversity goes,

Kniphofia northiae growing at Terra Nova Nurseries, Canby, Oregon.

there are dozens of species, mostly from South Africa. But in spite of their southern hemispheric upbringings, cold hardiness prevails reliably through zone 6 and occasionally colder, depending on how acclimated the plants are. Plant breeders have rolled the dice on new pokers lately, particularly Terra Nova Nurseries with their Glow and Popsicle series. Each of the glowers and popsicles offers a spectacular flush of flowers, often successively, on a dwarf (compared to their forebearers) though still dramatic scale. These forebearers too make great garden plants, growing into mammoth confabs of grassy and palm-like foliage with torchlight flowers. *Kniphofia northiae* has bodacious rosettes that burst into flower with orange and yellow battering rams in mid- through late summer. This species nestles itself amid boulders along streamsides in the wild but seems to thrive in a variety of soils in gardens, among the least fussy of the red-hot pokers.

On many trips south and west, I've encountered *Lobelia laxiflora*, and on every occasion have lusted for what I couldn't grow (seeing as it's only hardy through zone 7). Most charmed by the flowers—festive displays of candy corn and red hots—I've been equally impressed with its adaptability: this plant looks just as fine in Oregon as it did in North Carolina and Texas, regardless of the sun exposure or soil type. Full throttle, its flowers sizzle through high summer in defiance of burnt nothingness.

Kniphofia 'Ember Glow' stokes the fire well into autumn with citrus profusions of flowers on stems barely a foot tall.

(left) *Lobelia laxiflora*.

Gaillardia aristata (coll. 11SD3-NAB141).

For years, there was no love lost between me and blanketflowers. Despite their colors (which make them proud garden pennants of my alma mater, Iowa State), I just didn't dig them. Too many of the seed strains lack charm or presence—they melt in the summer, fall apart into a disheveled mess by fall, and reseed on top of each other, resembling an unruly mosh pit. Blech.

But then somewhere around 7,500 feet in the Black Hills of southwestern South Dakota, I had an epiphany. I encountered *Gaillardia aristata*, one of the truly perennial species of blanketflowers, growing by the zillions in amber and melon shades. I was hooked. What if blanketflowers could be true perennials, unlike the half-hardy, mother-was-an-annual-and-daddy-was-a-perennial wannabes I'd previously known? One free-spirited form I collected there flowers for months, often from early June through early September, and maintains a groundcovering habit that supports wiry antennae with rays and discs modeling the part of a fresh peach. It's proving an intriguing parent—the seedlings boast similar habits and inflorescences. Similarly, 'Amber Wheels', frizzled and fringed, rolls out its golden flowers for months each summer—a new introduction of merit.

Along about that time a blanketflower with real spunk, a yellow yowler that does everything to earn its name ('Moxie', no less), made its way into my garden. It's from John Dixon's Pandemonium Plants, and it

(clockwise from top left)

Gaillardia ×*grandiflora* 'Moxie'.

Cuphea 'David Verity'.

Gaillardia aestivalis var. *winkleri* 'Grape Sensation' at the JC Raulston Arboretum, Raleigh, North Carolina.

Cuphea 'Strybing Sunset'.

surely does have the potential to cause a stir. 'Moxie' is an all-star, regularly flowering from mid-May through frost, even without supplemental watering. Though in the heat of summer its effusion of flowers may not equal its spring and fall displays, its ever-present radiance is hard to deny. Flowering effortlessly in bright exposures and decently draining soils, it's a fluted charmer, evoking the memory of the popular 'Fanfare'. And its architecture? Mounded, compact, and superb—no flopping or flailing with this one.

For something completely different and yes, entirely un-photoshopped, 'Grape Sensation' offers a head-turning twist on everything we think we know of blanketflowers. It was selected from the Texas endemic *Gaillardia aestivalis* var. *winkleri* by Dawn Stover at the SFA Mast Arboretum in Nacogdoches. Exceptional in almost every detail, its abundant flowers prevail from late spring up until frost. Hardiness remains untested, though likely to at least zone 6, if not colder, without difficulty.

Common names don't do much except provide the illusion of making plants easier to talk about, and that's fine. In our efforts to avoid Latin, sometimes we just muddle the message. Here, we got it right. Firecracker plant. Done. *Cuphea*, the genus of subtropical shrubs and herbaceous perennials (so often grown as annuals in colder climates) with cigar-shaped, bat-eared flowers, has come around. In zone 7 and above, these flaming embers continue to earn a reputation for tenacious constitutions, wing-spreading architecture, and turn-crank floral displays that make other plants look bad. 'David Verity', a two-foot-tall and -wide hybrid of the shrubby, many-flowered *C. micropetala* and the low-growing *C. ignea*, just won't stop spitting out its hot little tamales, whether grown in Georgia as a landscape shrub (where it just keeps getting bigger) or in Chicago as a container feature. Hardy to zone 8, it prefers consistent moisture and a bit of shade but will do fine in short dry spells and full sun.

If you're blessed to live in zone 9, you should grow *Cuphea* 'Strybing Sunset'—no excuses or exceptions. Amounting to a compact, floriferous shrub in said climate, 'Strybing Sunset' is an amiable, affable plant for the mid-border mostly thanks to hundreds of tubular, orange-zest flowers. For the rest of us, it's a head-turning container plant, dressed with citrusy pizzazz.

SUMMER BULBS

Like flags of the season when phloxes roll into daylilies, a whole stable of summer-flowering bulbs augment the reality of that most of us call summer. Top of mind are gladiolus, even if nobody seems to be planting them. Gladiolus have sulked in the horticultural doldrums for decades, even as a murmuring resurgence of interest has slowly begun to change a familiar flower into a thoroughly modern Millie. The newest hybrids (almost all of which hail from eastern Europe, where the genus is having a heyday) verge on surreal—flamboyant bicolors in chocolate milk and lime, complete with eyespots and flecks, too. I'm not kidding. But amid this spasm of new colors, a return to the progenitors is underway, with gardeners reveling in the rediscovered hardiness of antique varieties.

'Atom', a 1950s-era cultivar, is as ruby as a flower can get. It's proven hardy in a smattering of locations north of zone 7 but not reliably enough to warrant an endorsement. Even if it's not a perennial, it's worth tucking into the border for July fireworks.

'Boone' is a new classic, named for its discovery near the North Carolina town of that name by NCSU extension agent Jeff Owen. It's a hybrid of *Gladiolus dalenii*, either escaped from the garden or hatched in the wild post-flight. Others like 'Carolina Primrose' butter up the color, where 'Boone' is just peachy. It's vigorous and that's an understatement, even in the cold nether regions of zones 5 and 6, where it will reliably overwinter, especially with some mulch. The definitive hardy glad.

One group of plants turns up again and again in the journal of my travels. It's that florist's heartthrob of a genus, *Alstroemeria* (Peruvian lilies). A few plant breeders have taken an interest in their perennialization (at least for northern temperate gardens), chiefly Mark Brigden at Cornell University, though they get less fanfare for their efforts than deserved. What's not to love about these plants? These temperate perennials have all the grace of a florist flower and bloom from late summer into fall. The genus itself, which does indeed hail from the Peruvian Andes, holds some wild and crazy members, hell-bent on growing in nothing more than chalky rock outcroppings—nothing close to the average garden's soil—with flowers that barely resemble their florist shop relations. Alas, they are botanical novelties, best consumed in online image searches.

Brigden's hybrids, though, are fashionable, stout, and hardy through zone 6a(5b). 'Freedom' poses liberating pink flowers on two-foot stems. 'Sweet Laura' flowers at thirty inches tall, its concoctions of golden orange flowers with darker freckling held atop a well-mannered clump. Others from Dutch breeders Könst Alstroemeria, chiefly the Inca Collection, are hardy to zone 5b, forming clumps with three-foot-tall stems, though I've found that flowering height often depends on the severity of

Gladiolus 'Atom'.

Lilium 'Debbie'.

(opposite top) *Alstroemeria psittacina* 'Variegata'.

(opposite bottom) *Lilium* 'Robina'.

winter, at least in the prairie states. Climates with perennial snow cover will benefit from the continuous insulation. 'Koice' (Inca Ice) offers quiet pink flowers borne in muted trumpet clusters.

Though less hardy than the newer hybrids, the white-edge princess lily (*Alstroemeria psittacina* 'Variegata') is among those most amenable to cultivation, provided you're gardening in zone 6b or above. Vigorously overstated in some boroughs, it's escaped into the wild in Mississippi and Louisiana, at least according to herbarium records (yeah, alright, whodunit?). Making lemonade from lemons, it makes for an undeniably tough hellstrip plant. Florally, who could resist masses of lipstick red flowers (even if they look hastily blotted or, worse yet, smeared) over white-margined variegated foliage? I can't. En masse, a clump will reroute hummingbirds.

On a more traditional lily bent (*Lilium* to those keeping track), Oriental lilies and their derivatives the Orienpets (perfumed hybrids of classic Oriental lilies like 'Stargazer' and long, white, bell trumpets like *L. longiflorum*) make summer worth living. On a humid, balmy summer evening leading up to a thunderstorm, the flowers emit a heavenly scent. 'Robina' is a hulking seductress with sturdy trunks up to five feet tall supporting bevies of pendent pink flowers, from which both color and nectar drip; the flowers have amazing substance, appearing to be cut from hard plastic. And the downward-facing flowers of the Orienpet hybrid 'Debbie', drooping from stems pushing past six feet tall, likewise

Lilium 'Lankon'.

pour heady perfume onto the garden scene below. Orienpet lilies take a few years to attain such scale, which comes with the added bonus of more and more stems.

Pioneering work to produce interspecific lily hybrids continues, combining disparate geography, genomes, and aesthetics to the gardener's delight. Tearing up this scene is 'Lankon', a 2011 release first shown at the Chelsea Flower Show. The name betrays half its pedigree: it's a laboratory-born love child of *Lilium longiflorum* and a Chinese turk's cap lily, *L. lankongense*. Sometimes plant breeders are clever like that.

Even with a mind left reeling at the beauty of modern hybrids, one cannot help but notice that their species ancestors offer charismatic flowers and simpler proportions. Among my first encounters with species lilies were the two prairie natives, *Lilium michiganense* (Michigan lily) and *L. philadelphicum* (wood lily), both named for places beyond the haunts in which I hunted for them. In the case of the latter, its common name suggested a clue for where to look, though it's by no means a lily keen on much shade directly overhead. Flowering at the margins of a woody draw on a prairie near my home, a stand of shocking red-orange wood lilies hovered just over their grassy counterparts. They looked out of place, and it's that memory I treasure, the pleasure of encountering something unexpected and so beautiful. In the garden, however, they are intermittent and fussy—my almost annual attempts to grow them

Lilium 'Larissa'.

have been perennial disappointments. Their colors shift across the two-thirds of the North American continent on which they occur, varying from red to orange to almost peach as they climb into the foothills of the Rocky Mountains. In that climate, strangely enough, they seem more amenable to cultivation; they are perfect in rock gardens with cool shade, forming handsome colonies that incite envy.

Of course there are lilies for shade—the martagon lilies kick off the summer garden even before the Orientals and other Asiatics begin to flower. Just when June is busting out all over, its dangling, recurved flowers appear, curled confections in ruby, orange, cream, yellow, pink, and blends in between. With so many buds per stalk and so many stalks, these hardy perennials ably join with hostas and ferns, hitting their summer stride, for a three-week affair every season. *Lilium* 'Larissa' is a martagon hybrid with *L. tsingtauense* ancestry. Canadian-born, this tough lady of the north boasts over thirty bright yellow bells per stem.

In comparison to all the fussing I did over wood lily, its Michigan counterpart was a cheap date. My original planting still thrives in its maiden location under the high canopy of a century-old bur oak, almost ten years after I committed two or three scaled bulbs to the ground. It does so well because it is in bright shade; introduce too much shade, and you'll slowly thin the ranks. In the wild, the species colonizes sloughs bordering wet prairies, a perfect indicator of where to put them in the

Michigan lily (*Lilium michiganense*).

garden: near enough to water that their feet won't dry out, even though they possess remarkable drought tolerance. As with wood lily, *Lilium michiganense* varies in color from orange to red, in either instance with intense vibrancy. After a few years, if you're lucky, your original bulbs will have sprouted stolons and run along to a spot nearby to plant themselves. I find their polite hiding-and-seeking endearing.

AUTUMN

Autumn is for the winners, a victory lap after the season past, no matter how hard the race. Colorful leaves (even a few), migrating birds (if hurrying along), cool temperatures (cooler still), plus colchicums, reblooming irises, and a host of other self-absorbing minutiae annually consume me. Yes, I'm in love with fall. Making a four-season garden has less to do with finding plants that look good in four seasons and more to do with taking cues from what's available in the season presented. It's these details—final flowers, ripening berries, changing leaves—that carry the garden through the fading blur of summer into the treasured but ever-shortening days of autumn. These short days are fine for planting, too. Annually, ritualistically, I plant bulbs, otherwise known as my shameless indulgence of the Dutch ancestry I don't have. Planting bulbs affords the gardener the hedonistic pleasure of digging many

Colchicum speciosum.

holes, spade slipping through the rind of the earth to round out a suitable pit. How you do it and what it looks like doesn't matter as much as how many plump bulbs get eagerly tucked inside the crater (yes, crater, because sometimes the zealousness of digging overcomes you). As you lie on your stomach, arranging them with care, the dream of spring seems tethered to the decisions of the moment—dirt under fingernails, hands cultivating the promise of life.

The fall crocuses, *Colchicum autumnale* and *C. speciosum*, are underplanted classics. 'Dick Trotter' should be grown more widely for its alarmingly high contrast flowers—white bases join vivid violet that looks smashing underneath a fully fruited beautyberry (*Callicarpa*). 'Waterlily' is another classic and an heirloom at that, introduced in the 1920s to the feverish acclaim of collector gardeners ever since. Collectors alone shouldn't hoard them, even if the plant's novel, mishmashed flowers look like a prom queen at the after-party.

EMBLEMS

Lycoris ×squamigera.

(opposite top) *Lycoris radiata.*

(opposite bottom) *Lycoris ×albiflora.*

AUGUST RUSH

In northern climates, autumn arrives on the fleeting gesture of an evening breeze in August, just as temperatures roll past their season highs on the downward slope to cooler, shorter nights. Autumn, in the broad sense, can last for months or be just as reluctant to stay around as it was to arrive. With such an unpredictable window in which to revel, I love to chock the garden with fall flowers—the dessert of the gardening season, the best for last.

The surprise lilies and naked ladies (*Lycoris*) are probably the first fall-flowerers to come to mind. Readily grown in zone 6b and above, they are already one of the more familiar passalong plants throughout the South and, deservedly, are picking up a larger following with each passing season. Lycoris are admired for their deer resistance and dogged persistence, and many blossom in the autumn as an overture to evergreen, understated foliage. *Lycoris radiata* is a red-light vixen with unsparingly colorful flowers. Most forms illuminate otherwise dim parts of the garden on fifteen-inch stems in mid- to late fall, not particular about soil as long as they get enough sun. 'Fireworks', a dwarf variety from Japan, should sell well for its name alone.

The first time I saw *Lycoris ×albiflora* in full bloom, I dropped to my knees in awe—a white surprise lily, indeed. Like hand-carved ivory tusks with whiskered appendages, its reflexed petals and exploding stamens could have eloped with the air if they weren't tethered in tight bouquets to fifteen-inch stems. It was naturalized in a shortgrass meadow garden, along a row of live oaks; perfectly situated.

Both deer-resistant and drought-proof, *Lycoris ×squamigera* is the lycoris of note in any garden north of zone 6, given its need for a cold vernalization in order to flower. With more common names than polite conversation can handle, this showgirl kicks off fall and persists into September. A sterile hybrid, it expends its energy in vigor and profusion, often outlasting by decades the gardener that plants it. The story of their life cycle is a classic romance of the gardening canon: lush, wide-bladed leaves emerge in the spring, only to disappear, forgotten—until two-foot stalks shoot up seemingly overnight. Pink flowers tinged neon blue light up not only the woodland garden but the hellstrip, mixed border, or just about any place you can stick in a shovel.

For whatever reason, I link *Lycoris* and *Rhodophiala bifida* (oxblood lily) together in my head. Another autumn harbinger, this Argentine native is consistently one of the most durable bulbs in the southern garden—alkaline soils, heat, and all. Like its garden mates, the oxblood lily falls asleep in spring after an evergreen endurance of winter. Then in late summer, fifteen-inch stalks erupt into amaryllis clusters of sanguine flowers. 'Hill Country Red', the popular garden form seen throughout most of Texas, was introduced by German settlers in the 1850s and passed along since.

Half the fun of the August rush is the notes of spring that seem to creep in. Take *Clematis heracleifolia* (bush clematis), which sidesteps the normative definition for the genus—thou shalt bloom in spring and summer—and flowers instead in late summer and fall. Adding to their transgressions, these bold clematis are both herbaceous and non-vining, among the easiest of these shrubby perennials, which emerge late in spring. Take note of their habit: they aren't floppy but lax—wide-shouldered, even. They benefit from a shoulder to lean on or a trunk to clamber upon (a nearby calycanthus or weigela will do). Habit aside, their sequential flowers, which open up over many weeks, do more than reward by appearance alone. Each upturned, faux-hyacinth flower exudes rich perfumes, varying by cultivar and provenance. At one time, I grew seven distinct forms, each uniquely scented with fragrances ranging from lemon to gardenia. In a word—profound. To think these are clematis!

While many cultivars are available, some stand out from the bunch, leaving the pundits to argue about their purported ancestry. 'Cassandra' grows to three feet tall and sports two-inch wide, honey-scented blue flowers. 'China Purple', another form often distributed, is more violet than most with somewhat smaller flowers (or at least a floral effect that seems muted in comparison). 'Davidiana' and 'Wyevale' are considered to be true selections of the species, and the former is credited with giving rise sometime a century ago to *Clematis ×jouiniana* (*C. vitalba* takes paternal responsibility for said hybrid). In the garden, try 'Mrs. Robert Brydon', an Ohio hybrid from the mid-1930s. I grow a particularly rich blue-flowered form of *C. heracleifolia*, raised from seed by my friends Caroline and Steve Bertrand of the Perennial Flower Farm. Its cobalt blue color bests 'Davidiana' in saturation and intensity.

To any seasoned gardener, windflowers (*Anemone ×hybrida*) are familiar plants, gracing the autumn garden with windswept, breezy charm. However, in spite of their airs, they seem to have fallen out of favor with new gardeners. If they make their way into new landscapes at all, it is rarely through the front gate in a black plastic pot. Rather, they're shared and passed over the garden fence—the sure sign of a plant that's either attained staple status (everyone is growing it, and if you're not, well...) or lost its favor over time. Anemones seem to have fallen prey to the latter. Gardeners in the late 19th century found windflowers incredibly fashionable, forcing the market to offer countless variations, somewhere around three hundred or so. Barely thirty remain in commerce, and even the most astute plant collectors would be hard-pressed to find them all available in one growing season. Still, I sense a renaissance. They're fall fabulous in every sense of the phrase, often flowering for up to two months, reseeding ever so nicely, and look great as a cut flower stuffed effortlessly into a vase sitting on the kitchen table—a stroke of instant decorating. In contrast to the usual hot colors

Oxblood lily (*Rhodophiala bifida*).

(right) *Clematis heracleifolia*, Perennial
Flower Farm form.

Like most windflowers, *Anemone tomentosa* 'Robustissima' is of desirable vintage.

of fall, windflowers blow through the garden in chill pastels—blushed pink and lavender to antique and crystal white. Perhaps unsurprisingly, most varieties still on the market are quite excellent, historical holdovers prized for easy flowering and carefree vigor. To name-drop a German trio—'Prinz Heinrich', 'Königin Charlotte', and 'Kriemhilde' sport whorls of ruffled, semi-double flowers that impose their silvered lavender and pink flowers on the burnished golds of *Solidago* with impunity.

The final flourish of the August rush comes from the pea family in my garden, an overt fountain of the fuchsia-colored blooms of Japanese bush clover (*Lespedeza thunbergii*). This plant suffers the fate of so many fall flowers: it's woefully ignored, simply because it doesn't look good in a nursery pot in May—the tyranny of spring. On a late August visit to a garden center west of Indianapolis, I encountered a huge specimen, probably eight feet tall in full flower. Chuffed, I asked the owner how well it sold. She chuckled and said that most customers never had the opportunity to witness it, much less purchase it, since so few people plant perennials in the fall (in her area). A tragedy in proportion to the perennial in question! Your garden needs one, but give it space. Its size, in October, suggests that it's some strange shrub, but by next spring, it will have disappeared almost completely, only to emerge with silver-tinted leaves through the remaining whipsticks of last season's growth.

Lespedeza thunbergii 'Samindare'.

There are more than a few cultivars, even if most look the same, varying ever so slightly in their degrees of pink and purple. Of these, 'Gibraltar' tops the honor roll. It's a waterfall, bowling over itself in a blooming profusion that steals the spotlight from anything else in flower. I wouldn't garden without it. 'Spilt Milk' lives up to its name, a splashily variegated selection of Japanese provenance that adds a dash more interest to this one-off emblem of fall. What's more, it's a dwarf, reaching only four feet in spread, about half that of the others. 'Samindare' is another fine fountain with exceptionally rich, lipstick-shaded flowers.

ASTER DISASTER

Chief among autumn's desserts are the asters—broadly speaking—though they are often denied the pomp and circumstance of a garden homecoming. Instead they sulk, unseen, in prairie remnants, ditches, and bygone places, raging against the season's dying light with shimmering rays of color. Designers of the New Perennial Movement use them to acclaim but even then favor a few species and cultivars that only scratch the surface. The impact of asters on gardens is vast—as a whole, most grow easily, in an endurance-testing array of variable soils, offering up flowers from midsummer through frost. For any of the autumn bloomers, a hasty buzz cut at the equinox usually keeps them in shape, lest they grow to unpleasing proportions.

In 1994, a group of well-intentioned botanists exploded the genus *Aster* (along with many other genera in the aster family) into a whole mess of names that bring to mind medical conditions or things you'd only talk to your psychiatrist about. The papers basically retained the name *Aster* for daisies of the Old World and threw a Latin dictionary at the North American natives, resulting in *Symphyotrichum, Eurybia, Ionactis, Ampelaster,* and others. Free advice from one gardener who happens to love plant systematics: live with the name changes and keep on gardening; they represent progress toward a better understanding of the botanical world. (I'll be the first to admit, though, that *Symphyotrichum* sounds like a third-world folk instrument and that *Eurybia* sounds like something you could have frozen off at the doctor's office. But we'll manage.)

Many, many cultivars of *Symphyotrichum novae-angliae* (New England aster) and *S. novi-belgii* (Michaelmas daisy) offer themes of purple, violet, and magenta, though most have a public nudity problem: they often lose their lower leaves by the time they flower, revealing bare, brown stems. If you're the type to expect a certain amount of public decency in your garden, you'll want to get creative with your "underplanting" or keep reading for alternatives. There's more to asters than these drag queens with hairy legs and purple top hats would suggest.

Starting with the seen and unseen—the seedy but rewarding *Symphyotrichum ericoides* and its vanilla-scented relative *S. pilosum,* the familiar heath asters. An inhabitant of old fields, roadsides, and prairies, *S. ericoides* is a rough and tumble aster that holds out in everything from dry, sandy soils to heavy clay, the latter of which makes a poor seedling bed for the 14.8 million seeds that seem to shed from each plant (kidding, sort of). But don't let me paint the wrong picture here—in a garden, densely planted, the seedlings really aren't too much trouble, especially if you've got the ground amply covered. In a garden, crafted in the nether regions of where gardens can be made, it's the surefire savior of any attempt at fall flowers. Architecturally, this aster can look like a bonsai or a perfect meatball, and anything in between, often with

The argent seeds of *Aster sedifolius* 'Nanus' (dwarf Rhone aster), in my scree garden late in the year. A knee-high specimen with twinkling lavender flowers, this European native is in fact a true *Aster* species and a delightful addition to any dry garden, even in the aftermath of its autumn show.

vegetation all the way to the ground. One outstanding variety, 'Snow-drift', never gets more than eight inches tall and instead billows out of the ground and over the edges of walls, sidewalks, or boulders in the most smashing way—a snow storm of tiny daisies in September. Don't care for white? A few pink forms exist, including 'Pink Star', which stays a bit more compact than the usual suspects.

All that said, I have to give a nod to the hybrids between and involving these two species because really, these freewheeling natives know how to have a good time, and the resulting plants defy description. The coveted amethyst aster (*Symphyotrichum ×amethystinum*) is a rare and naturally occurring hybrid between *S. novae-angliae* and *S. ericoides*. I've had the pleasure of searching for this plant in the wild, with no success, but that hasn't stopped me from attempting the cross myself in hopes of finding that one-in-a-million plant worth greater distribution and fame. Picture it—a million tiny flowers, just like daddy, all colored blue, like momma. An explosion of a zillion blue daisies held in fine array? Would you need another autumn flower?

If you're not for having just any roadside weed in your garden and still need something close to a zillion blue daisies, why not plant pine-scented aromatic aster (*Symphyotrichum oblongifolium*)? With lavender to periwinkle flowers, a rounded mound in full array rouses the sleepy bleached colors of autumn with a full-throated, heavenly hued exhortation. 'October Skies' and 'Raydon's Favorite' are two particularly fine cultivars of a species otherwise well-suited to dry soils. 'Fanny' and

A selection of *Symphyotrichum pilosum* I inadvertently collected (or did it collect me?) on a trip to western Nebraska. If given an inch, it'll take a mile—but what a show in September, when its scent on a warm afternoon triggers a sudden craving for sugar cookies.

Aromatic aster (*Symphyotrichum oblongifolium*).

(right) *Symphyotrichum oblongifolium* 'Dream of Beauty'.

its shrubby proportions should be planted as a hedge, if only to enjoy blue-violet waterfalls on the driest planting sites. 'Dream of Beauty' is aptly named—clouds of sugar-coated flowers adorn spreading plants half as tall but twice as wide as the previous two cultivars. South Dakota plantsman Claude Barr selected this pinky variant in the 1950s and it remains a vision of loveliness to this day, forming dense carpets of daisies that seem to thrive in sand or clay without fuss or disease.

And then there are moments when you can't help but curse the botanists who rename these plants. Who could imagine taking the descriptively christened *Aster azureus* (and damned if it ain't an azure aster) and calling it *Symphyotrichum oolentangiense*? What the what? Don't try to pronounce it out loud, lest someone think you've regressed into apehood. But don't let this detract from its endless list of garden qualities. Frankly, it's the epitome of the genus's attempts to outdo the waning colors of leaves. Aromatic aster might be nice, but this is nicer, though presented very differently—this time atop tall stems, perfectly suited for waving in taller stands of moor grass (*Molinia*) or wild rye (*Elymus*). Good for growing in dry soils, it will reseed gently if it's settled and thriving, which I consider a virtue. Butterflies flock to it in hordes, a spectacle of complementary colors—the rusty orange wings of monarchs thronging constellations of azure asters.

If you're limited to shade, don't feel oppressed by your lack of light. In the aster department, you have one singularly important choice—the durable, hard-nosed blue wood aster (*Symphyotrichum cordifolium*).

This is a plant long prized by native plant lovers but otherwise scarcely known. 'Avondale', a variety notable for profuse carpets of begging-for-bouquet stems, is the cream of the crop. Moreover, how can you pass up a plant that thrives in abundance in dry shade in September? What else is blooming?

The superlative selection of *Symphyotrichum laeve* is 'Bluebird' from Dick Lighty, formerly of the Mt. Cuba Center. Erect in habit, it's the stud of the fall perennial border, not flopping or flailing, all the while maintaining its leafy clothing. What's more, it's not fussy, thriving in a variety of soils.

And the options don't stop there. Have you ever looked at that bare trellis or wooden fence in the backyard and thought to yourself, "Now if only I had a *climbing* aster for that, I'd be able to sleep at night." You're in luck, insomniac! Meet the climbing Carolina aster (*Ampelaster carolinianus*), a southeastern native easily capable of five to six feet of growth up and along your favorite, uninhabited picket. Like its aster relations, it needs full sun and appreciates the company of nearby plants. It's a social butterfly, mingling and flirting with said company to the delight of the gardener, who'll hardly notice its bare stems as its heads enshroud themselves with icy pink blooms. The instant combinations are endless.

As with so many composites, the seeds of asters are elegant, softly puffy, and soon-airborne, and as with all dying perennials, their flaming foliage burns into the sunset in a final stand against frost. But one aster, *Symphyotrichum sericeum*, glimmers against the rest with silky, silver leaves and amethyst flowers. Admittedly a favorite sprig with rabbits in early spring when its silver strands shine the most, it's still one of my favorite asters. In flower, the plant is a collection of delicate tangles, adorned with daisy clusters—stems otherwise made for little girls and daisy chains. Sterling.

What would fall be without a host of other asters, like those from the genus *Boltonia*? Truthfully, there's not a lot to add about the emblematic charms of boltonias above and beyond the rest of the asters, save their glossier foliage and their general resistance to deer (so some claim). But one boltonia seems to command attention above and *below* the rest. 'Jim Crockett' is a blue-flowered and compact selection of *B. asteroides* var. *latisquama*, developed at the University of Massachusetts and named for James Underwood Crockett, the first host of PBS's *The Victory Garden*. Unlike its taller cousins, 'Jim Crockett' maintains its habit through the duration of its flowering.

Symphyotrichum laeve 'Bluebird'.

Missouri goldenrod (*Solidago missouriensis*).

TORCHES, FLAMES, AND FIREWORKS

Beginning in early fall, the temperate North American landscape shines in homage to the departing sun, particularly in the prairie states, where native plant communities dominated by members of the aster family take center stage. Next up? Enter goldenrods, wonderful natives which, as with the former *Aster*, have undergone taxonomic reorganization (almost as painful as it sounds) in recent decades and now belong to no fewer than three genera: *Solidago*, *Euthamia*, and *Oligoneuron*. Goldenrods don't garner much credit from anyone, particularly in the color department, given their themes and variations of gold and yellow. But chromatic limitations aside, their diverse floral geometry, plant architecture, size, and proportion more than make up for their monochromatic bent. Maligned for generations by gardeners with seasonal hay fever, goldenrod is innocent. Dastardly ragweed (*Ambrosia*) deserves the credit for such seasonal maladies; its pollen, unlike that of goldenrods, is light, readily wind-borne, and copiously produced. Bad timing, goldenrod.

The geometry of goldenrod flowers fascinates anyone who slows up the pace on a late fall garden walk. Botanists have taken note too, using this facet of their morphology to differentiate them. The shapes range from anvil and pyramidal to linear and exploding. Stiff goldenrod (*Solidago rigida*) pulls off a look that few plants do successfully—stark and rigid, yet graceful and understated. With its flattop yellow heads, it's the stoic beefeater of the fall garden. If you've always imagined yellow pipe cleaners in your garden, save the crafts for the kids and buy a few wand goldenrod (*S. stricta*); its incense-shaped flowers burn away the final days of autumn. I once had the pleasure of encountering the flaring spears of seaside goldenrod (*S. sempervirens*), which grows from Nova Scotia to the Gulf Coast, on South Padre Island. A species with striking adaptability to soil type—pure sand to silt loam—all the while enduring salt spray, its appearance in the wild, where it is dwarfed by its environment, barely hints at what it is capable of in the garden. Cultivated selections often double in size over their wild habits. Somewhere between flares and wands, the sparkling panicles of showy goldenrod (*S. speciosa*) entreat my attention, vigorously clumping into an October flame. Here stands a reminder of almost every goldenrod I've ever encountered in the garden—grow it leanly and without forgiveness. A little tough love goes a long way with a genus cussed for its aggressiveness in rich, composted soils.

Thread-flowered Missouri goldenrod (*Solidago missouriensis*) plays perfectly into any scheme that requires a spilling effect. I've not used it in a container, but I'm just goofy enough to try—imagine golden cords exploding into space like a handful of fireworks. In my scree garden, it mingles with California poppies (*Eschscholzia californica*) in cocktail colors.

Speaking of, no discourse on goldenrods could omit *Solidago rugosa* 'Fireworks' without some slight intended. Though fairly common, it's an essential plant in the autumn garden for its rugged beauty and seasonal regularity. Like the first pot of chili on a brisk fall day, you can't mark the coming of fall without a 'Fireworks' in full bloom *somewhere* in your yard. If you love the look of 'Fireworks' but want something a bit more rounded and compact, opt for the similar cliff goldenrod (*S. drummondii*), which incidentally is quite content to hang out in a medium-sized crevice along the driveway, if you happen to have one. Otherwise, a border, rock garden, or hellstrip will more than suffice. Cliff goldenrod never gets very tall (less than twenty-four inches if cut back in midsummer) but definitely takes advantage of the space around it with long, arching branches that reach to three feet in length. I originally put it toward the back of the rock garden, a decision I came to regret. It deserves to spill over the edge of a wall, much as it would in the wild, or grow in the center-of-attention mid-border, so long as it gets good drainage. Past its autumnal finale, I often enjoy the remnants of cliff goldenrod well into December and January as the tawny seed heads persist for months afterward. Resist the urge to hem it back in October, and you'll enjoy a bounty of winter interest.

All the goldenrods mentioned thus far thrive best in full sun. But what if you have only shade? Zigzag goldenrod (*Solidago flexicaulis*),

Cliff goldenrod (*Solidago drummondii*).

with its swanky namesake stems, prefers the coolness of oak trees and the closeness of toad lilies (*Tricyrtis*) over tall grasses and asters. I've been in love with this goldenrod ever since I first stumbled upon its curvy, crooked stems. For the coolest feature, look no further than its leaf nodes, where tiny rings of yellow flowers pop out in late summer and early fall. If you're in the market for a head-turning, fall-blooming native that thrives in dry shade, grab the cultivar 'Variegata', with its added feature of yellow-flecked leaves.

Helen's flower is no sneezing matter, despite its more common common name of sneezeweed. These perennial daisies are staples of the herbaceous border. Totaling more than forty species in the wild, the genus *Helenium* is home to some of autumn's best showstoppers, even if many begin in summer. A cheerful congress of cultivars exists, planting a dozen of which invites a continuous (with a little deadheading) parade of flaming, sizzling color from late summer through frost. Starting this parade might be russet-dappled and long-blooming 'Sahin's Early Flowerer' or crimson-tinted 'Moerheim Beauty'. 'Butterpat', an older Alan Bloom selection from the 1960s, is still around and is charming, a golden yellow early bloomer. If you're looking for something in the amber and orange realm try 'Wyndley' or 'Mardi Gras', both less tawny than 'Sahin's Early Flowerer' or 'Moerheim Beauty'. Tarrying on to the

Helenium 'Tijuana Brass'.

middle season of Helen's flower will be stalwarts like 'Kanaria', in bright canary yellow, 'Rubinzwerg', in rich red mahogany, and 'Waldtraut', a burnt yellow overlaid with orange. Many of the later-blooming cultivars are taller by coincidence. Those earning the distinction of being fashionably late are 'Flammenspiel' (an oft-times quilled red selection), 'Septembergold' (a clean upfacing gold), and 'Adios' (bright red).

The newest, hottest helenium is 'Tijuana Brass', a name inspiring the notion of a steamy, Latin night with bottomless margaritas. At five feet tall, it's a sunny flirt with sturdy legs, never falling or prematurely shedding its leaves. Introduced by the great plantsmen at Joy Creek Nursery, this rock star of dubious ancestry is sure to be a winner if enough people can get a hold of it.

If you know a thing or two about heleniums, you'll know that most of them are perennials, with one exception—*Helenium amarum* (bitterweed), which runs wild along the roads of the South and Great Plains. Up from the road ditch, this native annual is a smashing bedding plant in the landscape. 'Dakota Gold' offers tight mounds of golden daisies beginning their show in late spring and continuing through heat, drought, storms, and Armageddon until frost. This plant is essential, the glue that will keep your scree garden, gravel bed, hellstrip, or driveway border colorfully composed through the most vicious summer months.

Helenium amarum 'Dakota Gold'.

(opposite) *Rudbeckia subtomentosa* 'Henry Eilers'.

I couldn't imagine gardening without it. Oh, and you don't need an open garden to enjoy it. It's a versatile accessory in any container garden, whether paired for its feathery foliage or dapper daisies.

Topping my list of desert island plants is the now famous variant of the native sweet coneflower, *Rudbeckia subtomentosa* 'Henry Eilers'. Discovered by plantsman Henry Eilers in southern Illinois, this selection originally made the rounds thanks to Larry Lowman's Ridgecrest Nursery in Arkansas. Long a favorite of native plant lovers, it's ruggedly dependable in any situation. I grow it in a half-dozen places in my own garden, from near the downspout to the middle of the scree garden. The species' common name owes to the faint but detectable sweet scent that emanates on warm nights from the leaves and flowers (or whenever your nose happens to brush in close contact with the plant). Apparently in some climates with longer growing seasons, dear Hank outgrows his situation. (In northern gardeners, grown leanly, flopping is rarely if ever a problem.) Enter 'Little Henry', the halfling newer introduction with branched stems and just as many darling, quilled flowers. This is the wonderful nature of plantsmanship—for every taste, there is a menu.

Chrysanthemum ×rubellum 'Sheffield Pink'.

(opposite top) Chrysanthemum zawadskii 'Ryan's Rainbow'.

(opposite bottom) Chrysanthemum ×rubellum 'Will's Wonderful'.

ANYTHING BUT MUM

If you're like me, you're sick of chrysanthemums, at least the butch little fops sold at supermarkets in the fall. Bred only for their ability to fit tidily on shipping racks and with little more than a few weeks of worth, these plants are underwhelming. I want a mum that's anything but mum. I want a garden heavyweight that earns its keep season after season. No one-hit wonders either, please.

Taxonomically mums are a mess. Some place them in *Chrysanthemum*, others in *Dendranthema*. Whatever. Regardless, the so-called Korean mums (*C. zawadskii*) are drought-tolerant, hardy doers that have a history in gardens up and down the North American continent. In Atlanta at Oakland Cemetery, I admired 'Ryan's Rainbow', a strain distributed by Goodness Grows Nursery, via garden designer Ryan Gainey of Decatur, Georgia. A cheery array of flowers painted in a groundcovering mat on top of a stone wall—perfectly tough!

The antique mums of the early and mid-twentieth century were behemoths of perennial vigor. Most of them lie fallow in the compost of history, but like everything else vintage, a few of the old mums are making a comeback, distributed by nurseries passionate about authentic autumn showstoppers. But a word about the usual pinching—many of these heirloom mums don't need the usual midsummer snip that more modern hybrids do. Some are so late to bloom anyway that pinching would end flowers altogether—in cold climate gardens, they wouldn't have a chance of flowering before winter descended. While a few of the older varieties can get thin stems, staging them mid-border usually solves the problem. What's a little nudity for such a spectacular display, a renaissance tribute to a better era and stronger mums?

Chrysanthemum ×rubellum 'Will's Wonderful' is one such comeback kid. Garden writer Margaret Roach raved about it on her blog, *A Way to Garden*, in 2008, only to learn a year later that Seneca Hill Perennials had stopped carrying it (proprietor Ellen Hornig named the mum after the man who had passed it along to her). Well, it's available again, and it's worth saying that if you can have only one mum, Will is your go-to. It's often *the* last flower to show up in my Iowa garden, rounding out the growing season (even into November!) with showboat exposition.

Chrysanthemum ×rubellum 'Sheffield Pink' is another long and late bloomer, though you'll see it sold under a couple of synonyms (Hillside Pink Sheffield, Sheffield, namely). This variety benefits from a good pinch to reinstate its low, mounded, eighteen-inch-tall habit. Otherwise, it will need a companion to lean on when it's drunk with pink flowers in late fall (which isn't the worst of garden fates, provided the supporter has nice fall color and looks good with pink).

VIGNETTES

EXPRESSING YOURSELF IN THE GARDEN

**Personality is an unbroken series
of successful gestures.**

—F. Scott Fitzgerald, *The Great Gatsby* (1925)

At the juncture of environment, structure, and emblems comes the magic of making gardens: vignettes, a melding of essential ingredients into a stylistic personality that makes the garden your own. Marrying pairs, trios, and even menageries of plants is part of the hedonism of horticulture. In close proximity, in the frame of a portrait, these combinations are plant porn, stirring us with a shocking beauty that enthralls. It's these successive snapshots of personal expression, repeated throughout the garden, that make each garden a reflection of its creator. Repetition is achieved not only by using plants over again (which in so many ways seems absurd, with so many plants, so little time, and space ever shrinking), but by repeating the personalities and properties of the plants. Regardless of the feature—flowers, leaves, seeds, stems—the artfulness of plants in concert with each other is enchanting and tantalizing, so much so that it's worth starting with the ingredients and then finding the recipe. What gardener doesn't crave plant-driven gardens, rich with interest and passion?

The nodding flowers of kiss-me-over-the-garden-gate (*Polygonatum orientale*), an annual, repeat the arcing tracery of fountaingrass (*Pennisetum alopecuroides*), a perennial at Olbrich Botanical Gardens, Madison, Wisconsin. While neither are U.S. prairie natives, their spirit translates the emotion of a wild landscape into the language of a cultivated garden.

After all, the alternative seems almost nonsensical—what besides plants could drive a garden? The plants that power vignettes are those that deserve intimate inspection, their ambiance alive on a scale that demands daily consumption. Every plant tells a story, and each story connects us to the garden, the inspiration for which can come from anything. Diverse gardens are living communities, never static even if you tried to make them so. They grow and change daily, often in spite of their creators. Like a jazz pianist's riff, a gardener improvises within an acceptable framework, an artful style that embraces the evolution of circumstance and inspiration. The tricks to the riff, alive in the plants themselves, are straightforward enough: embrace the distraction of color, contrast everything, trust foliage, maximize plant personalities, and revel in what persists, the sweet endings of each plant.

THE DISTRACTION OF COLOR

Let's just get it out of the way: color is arresting. We love it. We plant for it. Gardens absent color, while perhaps populated with fascinating plants and interesting textures, are too often pitied for their reliance on green and rarely make the covers of elite gardening magazines. Colorful gardens, all things considered, are easy enough to cultivate with a deep deck of plants with style. Well-planted colors spark conversation. Mass effects are easy to plant and impactful, but beware the aftermath. Masses of flowers eventually give way to the mass absence of them. It doesn't take much to make use of flowers in full bloom. It's the after-party, when the colorful show has faded to memory, that requires finesse in the planning department.

Nepeta sibirica 'Souvenir d'André Chaudron'.

(opposite) The masses of pink used to great effect in the herbaceous layer thoughtfully echo the same colors occurring in layers much above the ground. In a sea of greens, the bristle brushes of *Persicaria bistorta* 'Superba' scrub the garden floor toward rhododendrons in the background, their colorful antecedents.

SUMMER BLUES

Blue is consistently the color that intrigues humans most, perhaps unsurprisingly because true blue is one of the rarest shades in nature. That rarity gives blue its allure. In the garden, blue is a charismatic color, saturating our imagination with dreams of beachfronts and the afterlife. It is perhaps most magnetizing in summer, when it's more unexpected than in spring. The catmints (*Nepeta*) inaugurate summer about as well as any blue-flowered perennial. Sure, they verge on lavender, blending shades between cultivars, even venturing into white and pink, but clouds of their classic flowers make up for a lack of color purity. Everyone knows and grows 'Walker's Low', and nobody argues that it's earned fan-favorite status. But there's more to catmints than sprawling blue mounds that flower forever until nobody notices them anymore. Newer varieties like 'Blue Lagoon', showing the influence of ultra dwarf *N. racemosa*, have sized down the same effect into something lower growing with frosty green leaves and plenty of blue flowers (note: the name 'Walker's Low' refers to the garden the plant was found in, not anything to do with its habit).

Many catmints in fact grow up instead of out. Some gardeners, mostly cat lovers, seem to find ornamental (or maybe it's purely pragmatic) value in growing *Nepeta cataria*, the wild catmint usually thought of as a weed. Believe it or not, cultivars exist, including 'Citriodora', which puts on quite a show of grayed lavender flowers (and has, as its names suggests, a citrusy smell). Nothing blue here. But if you're thinking blue (lavender blue) and upright, you should plant the bone-hardy Siberian catmint, *N. sibirica*, particularly 'Souvenir d'André Chaudron'. At nearly twenty inches tall and wide, it takes on a striking midsummer role in the perennial border with fragrance that *isn't* atrocious (at least to this human), as some catmints are. 'Souvenir d'André Chaudron' is strikingly similar to *N. yunnanensis* but with less of a habit for running and reseeding and more hardiness. The Japanese native *N. subsessilis* is quite nice, stockiest in habit of any mentioned here (up to thirty inches tall and half as wide) and with the darkest flowers. I'd love to see more breeding in catmints, but with so many fine examples, what stone is really left unturned?

Now for something truly blue—the Himalayan blue poppies (*Meconopsis*) of horticultural fable and lore. Volumes couldn't fully extol the obsession verging on lust that gardeners have had for these cover girls throughout history. Plants are notoriously difficult to germinate from seed, and many species are monocarpic, meaning they grow, flower, set seed, and die. Jerks. (At some point everything dies, but it'd be nice if they'd pay the rent more than once.) Neither characteristic has stopped plant hunters from traipsing into the wilds of Asia to describe and collect them. In the garden, the trick is mostly related to climate—cool, moist shade with a few hours of morning sun and no sweltering heat or humidity in summer, something of fiction for gardeners anywhere south of the Great Lakes or outside the Pacific Northwest. For the ultimate plant envy, visit gardens near Seattle or Vancouver or Quebec City (particularly Les Quatre Vents, known for *M. betonicifolia* by the thousands). Some things just aren't fair. If you're lucky enough to call these regions home, load up on organic matter and give them a shot. Fine strains exist, particularly 'Lingholm', a hybrid of *M. betonicifolia* and *M. grandis* with good perennial staying power, at least in the Edenic places amenable to their cultivation.

While long suffering from the reputation that they are difficult to grow, gentians have more in common with Rodney Dangerfield than Michelle Obama, and that's a pity. With nearly four hundred species from all temperate corners of the world, gentians can be anything from bog dwellers to scree settlers. Across eastern and central North America, many species of bottle gentians (*Gentiana andrewsii*, *G. clausa*, *G. catesbaei*) call wet prairies, woodland edges, and savannas home; few, however, seem to cross the garden fence into similarly styled planting areas. In late summer and fall, when their remarkably pure colors rage against the dying summer, gentians rule. For starters, 'True Blue', a hybrid from master plant breeder Darrell Probst, is among the finer new perennial releases in the last decade, despite its limited offering. The breeding behind 'True Blue' seems to have thinned out the fussiness of the species, while only amping up the blue rage with more intense color and larger flowers. A hybrid of *G. scabra*, the familiar rock garden gentian, and *G. makinoi*, a cold hardy Japanese species, 'True Blue' grows best in fairly normal garden soil and rockets into flower atop eighteen-inch stems starting in late summer.

If you have a knack for hypertufa troughs, the gentian palette offers plenty of choices. Any legitimate rock garden has at least a dozen forms of *Gentiana acaulis* (trumpet gentian), often due to their tendency to reseed into the gravel scree. While short and squatty, nothing dulls the brassy blue calls of a dozen flowers open at once. In spite of their rarity in gardens, trumpet gentians grow readily if given good drainage and bright exposures, and they weather drought with nary a missing flower. Urs Baltensperger of Edelweiss Perennials offers the best hybrids in the United States, selected for compact habits and luscious flowers, among them 'Renate' and 'Maxima'.

Gentiana septemfida is another of the dwarf gentians that thrives in more places than *G. acaulis* seems to. Readily adapted to hot summers in the Midwest and South, it's a welcome puddle of color in mid- to late summer. Avoid planting where taller plants would shade it out.

Salvia does blue as good as any genus can. In milder climates, *S. patens*, with its many large, claw-shaped flowers, borders on essential. Then again, in milder climates the salvia choices in general abound. *Salvia mexicana* 'Limelight' has a mile-long list of endorsements from esteemed plantsmen and garden designers. At six feet tall and wide, a well-grown specimen explodes with endless spires of blue flowers surrounded by lime green calyces. Cut them for bouquets and watch more stems replace them. It won't stop! The ultimate zinger plant—nobody

Salvia mexicana 'Limelight'.

(left) *Gentiana septemfida*.

Azure sage (*Salvia azurea*) backed up by the gold of fall at Olbrich Botanical Gardens, Madison, Wisconsin.

will miss this: it's a must-have perennial in zone 8 and above and an annual worth containerizing in colder climates.

Not all that's blue in salvias is left to warmer climates. Apart from the purple-blue hybrids of *Salvia nemorosa* that are abundant in gardens already (especially so thanks to their role in New Perennial Movement plantings in public spaces), several hardy blues are missing, among them *S. azurea*. Another late summer, often fall flower, azure sage pours out the flowers—a watery metaphor for a species that doesn't need water. It thrives on hot, dry sites, perfect for hellstrips and bygone alleys where concrete is more prevalent than chloroplasts. It's certainly more interesting than Russian sage (*Perovskia atriplicifolia*), but azure sage does have a tendency to flop in gardens, often because it's fed too well. Grow leanly and without charity. Nebraska plantsman Harlan Hamernik selected 'Nekan' north of Lincoln, a fine cultivar with lithe stems, tough constitution, and blue flowers up and down three-foot-tall stems.

If wetter planting sites prohibit planting fall-fabulous *Salvia azurea*, *Lobelia siphilitica*, the great blue lobelia of wet woodland edges and sloughs, would grow just as well. A clumper by habit, it thrives in consistently wet soils—the September highlight of the bog or water garden edge.

Great blue lobelia (*Lobelia siphilitica*).

(left) *Agapanthus* 'Queen Mum'.

On a more Mediterranean note, *Agapanthus* sings the blues happier than anything I can think of. Visually these plants are the perfect contrast—blue and dramatic, yet blithe and abounding. And while a few are white, deviation from the color norm doesn't change the point—in the open border or even containers, these things are fabulous. With so many varieties offered, it's hard to know where to start. 'Storm Cloud' and 'Summer Skies' gleefully take center stage in whatever large container you can find for them, handsomely accenting perennials with darker, moodier foliage to fashionable effect. The newer 'Queen Mum', a silver-headed ball of awesomeness, is destined to capture attention. I imagine them looking regal planted along a walkway or promenade, royally greeting everyone that strolled by. My hands-down favorite agapanthus, however, is *A. inapertus* ssp. *pendulus* 'Graskop', down but not downcast, beloved for its drooping flowers that are anything but Eeyore.

DELPHINIUM BLUES

Unless you're fortunate enough to garden in Alaska or similar cool-summer climates, forget about those dreamy photos you've seen—pillars of delphiniums floating above flawlessly kempt foliage. Such a look is unrealistic in most gardens, though a few of us remain hopeful (and will beat a staggering path to the compost pile in the process). Such is the gardening life (in denial). Yet, when I come to my senses, I'm satisfied with the progenitors of those colossal hybrids. They make life worth living, until we move to the Great White North.

Delphinium elatum, the Russian native behind all those hybrids none of us can grow, is the obvious place to start. This species offers many charms in its wild condition. In fact, it's damn lovely, owing its appeal to six- to seven-foot stems of cobalt flowers that rarely flop and a tenacious disposition that suits it to a scree garden as well as an overplanted perennial border. In retrospect, the only real upside to the hybrids are their denser flower stalks and larger flowers, which is all well and fine, but life is too short for everything in the garden to be big and blousy. Little, airy things deserve a chance to fill the voids, peppering the garden with diaphanous clouds of flowers that dazzle the senses.

Hailing from rocky bluffs in the Ozarks and Appalachians, *Delphinium exaltatum* vigorously thrives in moist to dry shade, owning the role of celebrity in the canopied garden. As its name would suggest, it commands exaltations, admired for its dressed-down simplicity, offering airier stalks of cobalt stars in contrast to Pyrex-blue beehives, which went out of salon fashion decades ago. Robust, blue-flowering, and shade-loving—how many plants top *that* list? Planted in rich organic matter, a clump will steadily colonize, thriving through drought and summer heat. Incidentally, the epithet *exaltatum* is Latin for "to exalt" or "lift up," which the plant does with fervor in bloom, bounding to three to five feet tall.

Delphinium tricorne flowering in an oak savanna remnant not far from my family's farm. It's most at home in the company of short grasses.

Finally, on the shorter end of things, two species merit consideration—the edge-of-woods *Delphinium tricorne* and prairie-style *D. carolinianum*. On their own, these larkspurs aren't that exciting—sort of like pasta with no sauce, not even butter and salt. Like many airheads, these natives need company to keep them from floating away into the Never Land between larger plants. Maximize their wispiness. Send them by the dozens into the mixed company of plants their size, and you've done well by them. *Delphinium tricorne* is slow to establish in gardens from seed but once it gets there, it dazzles en masse, blue stars at their shining best just above a plate of short grass. In contrast, *D. carolinianum* can grow a bit taller, more than a few feet, and self-sows to the delight of anyone who grows it. Even if it becomes weedy, there are far worse eager volunteers to contend with.

THE COLOR OF HEAT

The bench of plants tempting fate with devilish colors runs deep. Colors like these project energy and enthusiasm, daring to venture where most naturally occurring colors do not. If you need the wattage, there's no better place to start than the leaves of *Canna* 'Phasion' (Tropicanna). Just about every gardener has come across a canna at some point, mostly because it's hard not to. Heirlooms for well over a century in the United States, they were a familiar passalong plant in my family

It's a cheap trick, but few plants glow orange quite so well as *Canna* 'Phasion' (Tropicanna). Easy and available, its sensational foliage has made it a popular regular in gardens.

(right) *Canna* 'Blueberry Sparkler' offers alluring leaves painted in an unexpected hue. The flowers soften the psychedelic rave with a peachy reminder of normality.

growing up. Each fall when it came time to dig them up, I took a sort of huntsman's pride in mining their massive rhizomes out of the ground in search of that season's trophymaker. The genus has become a flashpoint for the nursery industry lately: a host of now widespread canna viruses (most notably canna yellow streak virus) have infected commercial supplies around the world. Tissue-cultured plants that have been virus-indexed are available but remain susceptible to any of the viruses once planted in the garden. All this hasn't stopped Brian Williams, owner of Brian's Botanicals, from introducing a spate of showy varieties, including the blue-metallic 'Blueberry Sparkler' and the drinkably delicious 'Lemon Punch' and 'Maui Punch'. These join the ranks of the already popular 'Phasion', planted abundantly (and justly so) for its otherworldly leaves.

With a common name like devil's tobacco, *Lobelia tupa* is almost requisite in any garden zone 8 and up that craves the burn. Flowering through the dog days of summer, this monstrous heat lover forms a six- to eight-foot-tall and four- to six-foot-wide clump that erupts into a spasm of red claws and hooks. This Chilean native, another plant that exacerbates my zonal denial, is definitely worth planting—if only for its impressive architecture at a time of year when rivals for attention are few.

Few plants manage heat as well as silenes, which I heartily endorse over almost any dianthus for that reason alone. In the same family, these kissing catchfly cousins may offer similar flowers in pinkish shades but part company in their tolerance of heat and humidity. In spite of so many superior traits, silenes have never gotten their due. The list of deserving varieties varies, depending on where you'd plant them. In the rock garden or front of border, *Silene* 'Rockin' Robin' (a selection from Thurman Maness) and 'Longwood' (a hybrid developed at Longwood Gardens by Jim Ault) have long topped my list of favorites. Sporting all the standard markers of hybrid vigor (including rampant growth rate and larger flowers), 'Rockin' Robin' politely screams at garden visitors in the most audacious shade of salmon. 'Longwood' takes its cues from childhood memories of bubblegum and cotton candy—softer shades but no less modest. Both are essential cushions of color in well-draining soils.

Silene regia (royal catchfly) is the reddest of the bunch, a prairie native that always reminds me where I have it planted when its flowers scream in midsummer. Reading between the lines, you'd gather that the plant has little to offer when not in flower—hide it amid some grasses, as it would grow in the wild, and let it lurk until it discloses itself.

On a September visit to the historic Santa Rosa home of plant breeding wizard Luther Burbank, I had my most memorable encounter with California fuchsia (*Zauschneria californica*), which was spilling from raised beds behind the house. I rounded a corner and happened upon its show: the flowers were the color of my cheeks, flushed with a smidgen of envy—we utterly lack something so scarlet in the cold north. This handsome U.S. native is among the best of the west, thriving in xeric conditions to the delight of anyone planting a waterwise garden. Its flowers are magnets for hummingbirds, its foliage a silver enticement for gardeners. Late summer and fall flowers occur with unrelenting profusion, burning through the long days of summer with scarlet trumpets outstretched from two-foot stems.

Zauschneria arizonica is a zone-5-hardy example of a genus that knows how to feed the flame. Up to three feet tall and two feet wide, this fall bloomer offers orangey flowers in comparison to its California cousin but does just as well on lean, dry soils. Cold hardiest in arid regions—winter wet is a prescription for failure.

I knew nothing of Uruguayan firecracker plant (*Dicliptera suberecta*) until I clicked through photos of its minted silver leaves and fire coral flowers on the Annie's Annuals website. Usually, the merest suggestion of southern hemisphere means this northern gardener might as well drop dollar bills down the drain. But for late summer containers, I knew I'd have the upper hand. If you garden warmer than zone 7a, you'll have excellent luck keeping it in the garden as a sprawling subshrub, never much more than two feet tall but easily three to four feet wide, if given the space to crawl.

(clockwise from top right)
Devil's tobacco (*Lobelia tupa*).

Royal catchfly (*Silene regia*).

Zauschneria arizonica.

Crocosmia 'Gold' (Twilight Fairy) represents a new era of dwarf, border-sized varieties, in this case with the added bonus of bronze foliage.

(left) I collected this form of *Liatris ligulistylis* (Rocky Mountain blazingstar) a few years ago in South Dakota, a petite dwarf with purple gumdrop flowers. While many forms flower near three feet, this front-of-border cheerleader makes do at just a foot tall in rocky soil and full sun.

Even though they weren't new to horticulture, crocosmias became pop culture icons in British gardens when plantsman Alan Bloom released 'Lucifer' in the 1960s. Fifty years later, they've gotten shorter. Sussex plant breeder David Tristram's 'Walrhead' (Little Redhead) dances in the devil's colors but at a mere twenty inches tall, in comparison to the towering 'Lucifer'. With months of bloom, 'Walrhead' and its bold bevies of saturated flowers deserve a front-of-border planting spot in any garden, zone 6b and above. The Twilight series from Terra Nova Nurseries puts a modern spin on crocosmias, tailoring them to the borders of modern urban gardens or the retro-vintage containers of decks and balconies. Many nurseries offer handpicked seedlings, but few have achieved widespread distribution, especially in the United States. In those colder zones (say zones 5 and 6, where it's still a gamble), spring planting yields the best results, giving the somewhat tender plants a growing season to establish and develop enough of a crown to last through whatever winter might throw at them. 'Distant Planet', an orange-flowered, three-foot-tall selection, reportedly overwinters in zone 5b without protection, though probably best so in climates with consistent snow cover. My own trials in Iowa haven't (yet) yielded a positive result.

Less about their colors and more about their name, the blazingstars (*Liatris*) may not bleed as sanguine as the rest, but their geometry, highlighted with fluorescent purple, makes them a standout in the summer heat. *Liatris spicata* (spike blazingstar) has grown in gardens for the last few decades, annually pumped out by the tens of thousands from the Dutch bulb fields. But there's more to blazingstars, though nothing really different in color (save shades and tones). Like their fellow aster family members the goldenrods, much of the fascination of liatris lies in the shape and construction of their flower spikes. Some are bauble-headed (*L. aspera*), others whipcords (*L. acidota*). Some grow wet (*L. pycnostachya*), others dry (*L. punctata*). To say they are versatile would be understating it. These North American natives flower on the tide of falling leaves, prepping monarchs and other lepidopterans for their southbound, thousand-mile trek—yet another reason to add them to any ecologically conscious planting scheme.

CONTRAST IN EVERYTHING

An essential and universal concept in design of any sort is contrast; in garden making, it concerns the appreciable differences between plant features. Traditionally, writers have used the word "texture" where I use the word "contrast" to explain the basic differences in the shapes and sizes of these leaves, flowers, seed heads, and the like; but there's more to contrast in the garden than a scale of size, and a better way to describe variance than using a word that many associate with touch. So, "contrast" it is. Contrast also exists in time and space. The value of manipulating plants in these dimensions is quite practical. Imagine something like a monarda that flowers beautifully in the summer months and then persists into another season. The seed heads lingering into September stand in contrast to the autumn garden—a juxtaposition of summer and autumn. Simply put, artful manipulation of contrast—exploring and extrapolating the differences between plants in the garden and over time—makes for dynamic gardens. Contrast gives the gardener leverage.

The importance of contrast would be obvious to us all if we could tune out the distraction of color. Our eyes are addicted to color, constantly processing droves of data which accumulates as white noise in our brain. Beyond the realm of color, though, lies a deep well of visual

Monarda bradburiana, the Ozarks' native horsemint, is fast becoming a patently essential plant in many modern gardens. It is the earliest bee balm to flower, ushering in the arrival of summer. After it senesces, the seed pods remain well into autumn, joined by the burnished royal purple leaves that come with the cooling nights.

(right) Ever in motion, the seasonal shift of summer to fall is striking: a transposition of green into yellow in just a few weeks. Chartreuse and filigree, the foliage of *Amsonia hubrichtii* contrasts always with the steely blue needles of the blue spruce, but joins *Hibiscus acetosella* 'Panama Red' in colorful conversation as it takes on golden hues.

In Decatur, Georgia, late in the fall, *Amsonia hubrichtii* serves as a foil for the generous fruits of American beautyberry (*Callicarpa americana*), clustering the lengths of six-foot-tall stems, a contrast in plants with dynamic seasonal expressions—spring and fall.

(opposite) Contrast rules supreme here, driven by the showy summery shields of *Zantedeschia*, speckled and peppered with silver. The silver draws attention to the dark-leaved dahlia hovering overhead, a theme gently repeated all along this garden border. Lithe, snaky stems that a short time ago bore the radiant orange of crocosmias dance aerially, adding another dimension to the already abundant textural and color contrasts.

The serendipitous stroke in this vignette? The silver plume of Louisiana sage (*Artemisia ludoviciana*) wandering through a perennial border of my youth. But in mid-August when this photo was taken (and really through the end of the growing season), that welcome silver filled an unlooked-for void. It's unexpected and that's half its success.

(opposite) This collector's garden holds hundreds of thousands of rare ferns from around the world. The distraction of full-color greens and browns, even if sublime, numbs us to the garden's nuances—in this case, revealed in black and white, the highlighted fans of *Sabal* palms.

stimulation. The shapes of green leaves might seem boring, but absent color, the magic of their geometry reveals itself.

The garden's bones benefit from a thoughtful and intentional consideration of contrast, but let's admit it: sometimes the quintessential element behind smart combinations in the garden is serendipity. Every fortuitous happenstance is a reminder that we never truly create anything in the garden but rather facilitate interactions and growth that often exceed (or simply defy) our expectations. Creating a garden that can reinvent itself through the biology of its components elevates simple planting to high art.

IN LEAVES WE TRUST

If flowers are obvious, leaves are overt, even if they too often go unnoticed. The modern garden is marked by its understanding that foliage—of all shapes, sizes, colors, and presentations—is the real undercurrent that keeps aesthetics afloat.

I'm a relative latecomer to tropical plants, perhaps because I was brought up in the Midwest, where the idea of planting big, waxy leaves in the garden seemed foreign beyond my comprehension. More than once my interior monologue went something like this: "If it's not hardy, throw it back," a comforting, comfortable thought, suggesting that the pool of plants I cultivated needn't include those a brutal Iowa winter would crush. I never had much of a knack for tropical houseplants either, much preferring to grow plants in the free outdoors than the ever-too-dry containers of my bedroom and living room. While I liked the idea of living among my plants, I'd just as soon live in the garden outdoors instead.

But nagging botanical curiosities crept up on me. I found that some plants were just essential to satisfying my inquisitiveness—gesneriads, aroids, tropical cactus, agaves, plectranthoids (I made that word up, but you get the idea). And while these were essential, the limitations of climate would otherwise prohibit most northern gardeners from growing them beyond a container, unless you're fortunate enough to grow agaves in your perennial border in zone 7 and above. Here sets in zonal denial, that horticulturally clinical condition of envying warmer winters, longer summers, and the unspeakable dozens of plants presently beyond your reach. There is no cure, but you needn't fight it. Some genera work famously as seasonal superstars.

The world of aroids—commonly called elephant ears—has its host of celebrities. As a descriptor of their size, big would be an understatement. Trying to spin out a list of top five favorites is pointless. At some point I realized that I generally didn't have a negative word to say about any that I encountered. 'Sarian' is a personal favorite for its windowpane-veined leaves, which are prisms to a photosynthetic universe. It's reminiscent of the golden-stemmed *Alocasia macrorrhiza* 'Lutea', though much more subdued than the glowing, banana-yellow petioles that rise from a center crown of the latter like praying hands. It's borderline reckless to throw a height rating for any of these. As tropicals go, these things have voracious appetites for any strong concentrations of organic matter thrown their way. Feed them, Seymour?

Another favorite, formerly quite rare, is *Alocasia odora* 'Okinawa Silver', the horticultural world's version of a Rorschach. No doubt it was one of the temptations that induced my tropical labors—its splashy, sexy variegation and incredible vigor rewarded my every effort. I've since shared it with many friends, who've shared it again. Like many aroids, plants are heavy feeders—fertilize and they will thrive (perhaps at the expense of your container).

New breeders and new varieties have added a lot to the market and put a spin on the plants that formerly were valued for their size and personality and less for their individual novelty. If his early introductions are any clue, Kentucky-based plant breeder Brian Williams is well on his way toward royalty status among aroid aficionados. His *Alocasia sarawakensis* 'Yucatan Princess' is both a mouthful and an eyeful. Grand and voluptuous, its soft but not muted colors of gray-green and milk chocolate play well with neighboring plants, while not overpowering the scene (anything more, given its size, might just be too much). In

The apple green veins of *Alocasia* 'Sarian' dam up plots of jade green, giving these monumental leaves their wowing appeal.

(opposite) *Alocasia odora* 'Okinawa Silver'.

a container by the door, it's a one-plant garden—at once minimalistic, modish, and stylish. In the *Colocasia* realm his most successful introduction to date is 'Noble Gigante', essentially a black-leaved form of *C. gigantea* 'Thai Giant', the favorite oversized taro. Growing as much as eight feet (or more) during a single growing season, a mammoth clump can stop traffic with an eruption of dramatic color and texture. This brings a whole new meaning to guerilla gardening.

John Cho's 'Black Coral', a metallic-leaved selection with high shine, is among the best in black colocasias for vibrancy and color. According to Tony Avent of Plant Delights Nursery, early name suggestions included 'Exxon Valdez', a testament to the plant's crude, sooty, lacquered (the adjectives could run on for pages) black leaves that fill out into a voluminous, three-foot-tall fountain. My go-to variety for container centerpieces because of its more modest size and vigorous growth.

Somewhere between tropical and desertified, yuccas occupy a space in the wild that translates beautifully to the garden. Around fifty species of these woody asparaguses (which is what they are, botanically speaking) call the western hemisphere home, growing from the High Plains (*Yucca glauca*) to the Caribbean (*Y. aloifolia*). While their magnificent

Yucca filamentosa 'Hairy'.

spires of white bells might charm us for a few weeks a year, it's the sharp rosettes of foliage that persist, always available as a counterweight to the parade of flowers passing by. *Yucca aloifolia* 'Blue Boy' (sometimes sold as 'Purpurea') found me in a nursery near Asheville, North Carolina, several years ago. This zone-8-hardy subtropical sports broad sword-like leaves blushed with purple and blue—an arresting specimen in containers for northern gardeners, or a slow-growing evergreen in mild climates. For the rock garden, forms of *Y. glauca*, *Y. harrimaniae*, and *Y. filamentosa* are desirable. *Yucca filamentosa* is a Midwestern native, occasionally found around abandoned farm sites, no doubt the fascinating prize of a pioneer gardener who made home beautiful with tough plants like this. A variegated form ('Variegata') exists, though it's rare in cultivation. It's more polite than non-variegated forms, which can rapidly colonize with thick woody stems, and it flowers just the same. A dwarf, excessively fuzzy clone is sold under the obvious name of 'Hairy'. At eighteen inches tall in foliage (and reaching up to a few feet in flower), it's a pip by comparison to its forebearer and couldn't have better proportion when planted along a sidewalk or path.

In contrast to tropical behemoths, I relish fine-textured leaves as a chef treasures threads of saffron—for so little added to the soup, the

With a name like *Acorus gramineus* 'Minimus Aureus', this petite golden form of sweet flag seems to have jumped right out of a Roman epic and into this garden crevice alongside *Sedum tetractinum* in Robyn Brown's Nashville, Tennessee, garden. This genius combination showcases the pairing power of just two plants in the same general color palette, as if to suggest that like a well-planned summer soirée, you really need only one good wine and one fine cheese.

(left) I can't get enough of the bronze sedges (*Carex testacea*, *C. flagellifera*, and cultivars) even if they are derided as the living dead. Such color, rare enough in plants, coupled with first-rate texture is worth every cross word. In this vignette along a busy driveway at Pleasant Run Nursery, Allentown, New Jersey, their metallic threads knit together the hot pink flowers of iceplant (*Delosperma cooperi*), the purple-touched leaves of *Viola walteri*, and a few spires of lavender.

Repeat personalities, not just colors, for a satisfying, unifying sense of repetition. Here, spicy hot flower spikes of *Persicaria amplexicaulis* 'Firetail' swim through like-shaped seed heads of *Pennisetum*. Two nearly equally charming personalities are married together, underscoring the elegant simplicity of making vignettes—less, so often, is more.

flavor improves tenfold. Fine-leaved plants often feature prominently in gardens, whether given full control of the stage as roving, thriving centerpieces or sited as appurtenances to more muscular plants nearby. In either case, in contrast to their surroundings, those filigree leaves tickle the eyes.

MAXIMIZING PLANT PERSONALITIES

Collecting, planting, and maximizing plant personalities—their particular aesthetic charms—is the truest expression of a gardener's self. Assembled into harmonious vignettes, they form the weft of the modern eclectic garden. And the dynamic natures of these personalities, in the snapshot moment and over time, are expressive in a way that words can't describe. Whether we stage them solo or en masse, on a small or large scale, it's our relationship with characterful plants that makes a garden personal.

DIVAS

In the world of plants, nothing is democratic—all plants are not created equal. Some are divas, stage-hogging rock stars who need their time and space to put on a show. Others are dancers, subtly flitting between their strident co-stars, just hoping to keep up. Yes, plant personalities scale along the lines of a casting call. The interplay between these characters makes for entertaining gardening.

It's hard to ignore the biggest personalities in the garden. Some plants have gravitational pull, owning the stage through the duration of their performance. They are loud in color, large in size. They are the stars, the talking points on a garden walk—they need to be shown off. Plants with black foliage are the ultimate punk divas, daring to challenge the green paradigm while simultaneously bewitching the soul. Effusing shades of purple and red that border on sooty and satin, the leaves of these punks stand out like a defiant hipster with too much eyeshadow—these plants beg for attention.

Actaea simplex 'Hillside Black Beauty' bowled me over the first time I discovered this drama queen in a garden—I mean, the first time I was in her audience. Bold and dramatic, there's nothing quite like a five-foot-tall vixen dressed in black to make your head turn. Late in the summer, white spires add to the stagecraft of this denizen of partial shade.

Effusing chartreuse is an equally punkish thing for a plant to do. *Kolkwitzia amabilis* 'Maradco' (Dream Catcher) gives most Tiffany lamp shades a run for money in terms of luminosity. In generic terms, it's a focal point, but planting one will do more than draw the eye in its direction. It will redefine the vignette, slowly growing into a five-foot-tall profusion of brushwood that breaks bud in spring to reveal little drops of acid green leaves burnished with a bit of bronze. As shrubs go—vase-shape, dazzling leaves, subtle flowers—this is the stuff of dreams.

One gardener's weed is another's weird and this weird weed is big. I happen to be a huge fan of the hulking framework of pokeweed (*Phytolacca americana*), which grows up to six feet tall and wide. Few perennials offer as much architectural interest as these botanical mobiles, especially the variegated 'Silberstein'. Cream-splattered leaves cloak purple stems until pendulous, tube-sock white flowers overtake the plant in late summer. Saving dessert for last, the inedible and highly poisonous fruits are juicy temptations for birds, but not until late winter, when their astringency has faded (though most have likely fallen to the floor by then). Weed out unwanted plants. As a variegated weed, I think it qualifies as an exception.

Some divas own the stage before they even leave the nursery pot. Harnessing their marquee personalities requires maximizing their physical stature and showcasing the boldness of their leaves and flowers as much as it requires an understanding of how they grow. Golden comfrey (*Symphytum* ×*uplandicum* 'Axminster Gold'), for example, emerges from a tough, densely budded crown that bulks up into a horticultural mastodon after years of growth. Its annual ritual of flagrant foliage succeeded by ascendant flower spikes quickly accomplishes the plant's evolutionary commandment: flower and get out of the way. Cut

(clockwise from top)

Actaea simplex 'Hillside Black Beauty' is the drama queen here. Oh, and her little sister? 'Black Negligee', a newer hybrid with lacquered black foliage and a slightly more compact habit. Both are essential divas worth top billing.

Kolkwitzia amabilis 'Maradco' (Dream Catcher).

Phytolacca americana 'Silberstein'.

Symphytum ×uplandicum 'Axminster Gold'.

(opposite) *Crinum ×digweedii* 'Bolivia'.

back in early summer, it returns for a reprise, a showy camp of leaves that last through early autumn. As a planting choice, it's a lamppost for shade vignettes, rising up from the garden floor in stark contrast to its companions.

Travel through the South in spring and early summer and it's hard to miss one of the horticultural hallmarks of the region—crinum lilies (*Crinum*). If ever there was a foolproof plant, crinums are it. Tough as nails, deer-proof, and boasting sculptural mounds of silvery green leaves, these ditch denizens not only offer striking foliage but blaring trumpet flowers in variations of peppermint, pink, and white. Beyond the shelter of zone 8, crinum lilies make zinger container specimens. As an aside, *C. bulbispermum*, one of the more commonly seen crinums with large, scalloped leaves of pewter green, will overwinter in zone 6 with protection.

Jenks Farmer, the *Crinum* dude by any estimation, is one of the genus' loudest champions. Almost any crinum I've come into contact with has been thanks to Jenks. One, *C. ×digweedii* 'Bolivia', is a stalwart of southern gardens christened with a new name for modern times. It flowers abundantly in late summer and into fall. I'm smitten with 'Menehune' (Purple Dream) for its seductive purple foliage set against radiant sprays of pink flowers. This Sean Callahan hybrid (*C. oliganthum* × *C. procerum* 'Splendens') may not make a huge play in the American market, given its limited hardiness (to zone 8b), but it's well worth

Aralia cordata 'Sun King'.

the effort to find one. This diva rocks both flowers and foliage, and it is small for a crinum, reaching only about two feet in height (hence Mene-hune, a reference to the mythological forest-dwelling "little people" of the Hawaiian Islands).

In rich, heavily composted soils, Sun King aralia can reach gargan-tuan proportions, topping out at over six feet tall and wide. In more modest fertility, it's a patient border plant, shin high and rounded in width. Siting it accordingly makes the difference between cussing it as a bully intent on clearing a way for itself or as a gracious superstar that knows how to support its cast. Exposure also effects its presentation—in full sun, it's golden, while in part shade it's lime. The proper place-ment of plants, regardless of the magnitude of their personality, goes a long way toward your ultimate enjoyment of them.

In my mind, true diva plants almost always offer more than out-landish foliage or flowers alone. But sometimes blatant flowers win the shouting match. Foxgloves, long overdue for a celebration, are now all the rage. No longer a relic of cottage gardens past, these charming, quintessential perennials have attained diva status, thanks in part to new varieties that have sauced up expired rhetoric about the value of these spiked plants. *Digiplexis*, the storied cross between *Digitalis purpurea* and *Isoplexis canariensis*, changed everything. It's not in fact a intergeneric hybrid; rather, in a shocking twist of chlorophyllic drama, its parents turned out to be cousins, closer kin than originally thought. But the name stuck, partly because it just sounds so damn cool. *Digi-plexis*. How Midcentury mod. The hybrid wasn't revelatory for its cool moniker though. It opened up an avenue of possibilities, demonstrating

Digiplexis 'Illumination Flame'.

that foxgloves weren't only those paisley-spotted purple things you saw tossed in the compost heap at the garden center (because who was really buying foxgloves?). The flowers of 'Illumination Flame' trump anything Grandma loved—thimble shot glasses of tequila sunrise that flow without end. Even the axils get in on the fun, sporting buds long into the summer after the initial flowers have developed. While it's hardy only to the balmiest corners of zone 8, additional generations of hybridizing have revealed hardier types, so keep your eyes open.

Digiplexis did nothing more than to shed light on its fellows, awakening gardeners to a tribe of great perennials that for too long had languished in obscurity. Funny enough, one even carried the Latinized form of the word—*obscura*. *Digitalis obscura*, which offers untold riches of yellows, coppers, and ambers, indeed is an obscure dark horse in a genus otherwise replete with purples, whites, and lavenders. Its flowers invite gawking, and its Spanish roots underscore an essential insight into its culture: while surprisingly hardy (zone 4), it despises wet soils, particularly in summer. In xeric gardens, thriving despite water restrictions, few plants look more at home. Deadheading encourages repeat flowering and reseeding, both of which are desirable.

What *Digitalis obscura* does for the heart, *D. ferruginea* does for the brain. It's like the bookish girl at the library that catches the attention of the all-star athlete, not because he's bowled over with beauty, but because she's interesting beyond a pretty face. *Digitalis ferruginea* (by another name, chocolate- or caramel-flowered spires of awesomeness) looks fetching in a border where it can rocket beyond its perennial companions to towering heights.

DANCERS

In contrast to divas, dancers hover at the side, the supporting characters without which the stage would be empty. These plants exist in the matrix of the garden, inviting discovery. They're not flashy by definition, but what they lack in bravado they make up for in charm. Their overall simplicity suggests a certain sophistication, a freedom to relish less in spite of more. Dancers that reseed and hover in the spaces between plants, even if they may momentarily dominate the scene with their chatter, are essential for adding grace and depth to the layers of a planting scheme.

Think of the burgundy bobbers of *Sanguisorba tenuifolia* 'Purpurea', draping elegantly over whatever grows below them. If you're looking for a color a little less subdued, say hot pink, why not employ the fuzzy locks of *S. hakusanensis*? Plants like this bring movement to the garden, nodding with the wind. Even the dwarf *S. officinalis* 'Tanna', a miniaturized version of its taller cousin, reproduces the effect on eighteen-inch flowering stems, hovering over delicate, feathery leaves at ground level—the perfect burnet for the small garden.

In my native haunts, purple prairie clover (*Dalea purpurea*) reliably explodes into violet bottle rockets, best set against a grassy green backdrop for the scene to have maximum effect. Retired University of Nebraska plant breeder Dale Lindgren developed the seed strain

Sometimes conversations occur between flowers of the same plant, as seen here in this flickering colony of Japanese primrose (*Primula japonica*) in the bog garden at Hatley Park in Victoria, B.C. Encourage reseeding in vari-colored dancers for this reason alone—variety is the spice of lively, expressive gardens.

Sanguisorba tenuifolia 'Purpurea' is an essential associate of bolder leaves and flowers in the high summer garden.

(right) Purple prairie clover (*Dalea purpurea*).

'Stephanie', to date the only named selection of this tough, broadly adapted prairie species worthy of greater appreciation in gardens. Purple prairie clover thrives in nature on a variety of soils, sand to clay, but in the garden seems to do best on the drier side. Amid the company of other plants, it lilts across the dance floor with titillating flair. Although slow to establish, the color tracing effect, a three-week affair in mid-summer, is worth the wait.

Some plants are airheads, supporting characters on an extreme of the dancer spectrum. Airiness in the garden isn't hard to come by, though it rarely shows up on the menu. What's not to love about a plant that knows how to manage its negative space? On the theme of airy, plumed, and less is more, prairie dropseed (*Sporobolus heterolepis*) flirts with invisibility on close inspection but makes up for it with many feathery tassels per clump. Most forms of the species spread widely when in flower; 'Tara', a dwarf cultivar discovered by plant whisperer Roy Diblik along the Kettle Moraine in Wisconsin, is the best choice for urban landscapes short on space. Or throw two or three airheads into the same vignette for a magnified mass of empty space, contradicted only by them crossing into each other. Consider how these three personalities interact with each other: Korean feather reed grass (*Calamagrostis brachytricha*), known for its stately plumes and ability to thrive in clay, can support both the upthrust flowers of *Cephalaria gigantea*, ovoid

Prairie dropseed (*Sporobolus heterolepis*).

(below) This combination of *Calamagrostis brachytricha*, *Cephalaria gigantea*, and *Lavatera thuringiaca* is breezy even without wind, a competing whirl of personalities held in common by their minimal intrusions into space. I'm smitten.

Anthriscus sylvestris 'Raven's Wing'.

discs flying through space, and the loosely clustered, lavender spires of *Lavatera thuringiaca*.

If only *Anthriscus sylvestris* 'Raven's Wing' offered some sassy, neon blue flowers against its remarkably saturated black foliage. But nature gave us white, instead. Despite my lack of enthusiasm for white flowers, I have to admit that the whole package this plant offers really takes my neurons for a spin—who could deny the seductive qualities of dark, lacquered foliage, offset by clouds of tiny flowers? If black foliage isn't quite your rage, you could easily cross-categorize this strong personality with other airheads, planting it for its contrasting haze at peak flowering. Like so many umbellifers—carrot family members by another name—the floral effect is as airy as it comes, even if they are biennials (though reportedly in San Francisco they persist for years). Now, biennials don't get a lot of love. It's puzzling—to be a horticultural favorite you either have to have a shelf-life of nine months or four years (or more) to get any kind of respect. Two-year affairs mean nothing. Where have we gone wrong? Do short-term relationships mean nothing nowadays? The beauty of so many biennials is that they freely reseed, perpetually setting off another cycle of short-lived but extremely satisfying two-year flings. As for 'Raven's Wing', this plant's hardiness is underrated, if largely untested. I've seen it overwinter in the Midwest in mild winters, though many nurseries list it as hardy only to zone 7.

Flowering spurge (*Euphorbia corollata*).

Someone needs to kill a few plants for the cause. I suppose if you're content to treat it as an annual for its rich flush of freshman foliage, nobody will judge you.

The familiar spider plants (*Chlorophytum comosum*) of dormitory fame have terrestrial cousins that are more apt to throw off tiny flowers than wayward plantlets. *Anthericum ramosum* grows from grassy crowns that flutter with starry white flowers in late summer. The flowers spray from wide branches atop tall stems, filling out into a slender profile about three feet tall. Apparently far more common in the United Kingdom than the United States, this Mediterranean native is a lost lover of rose gardens everywhere, which badly need accoutrements in the rose-waning days of July and August. Similar to gauras, though never pink, and in my gardening experience, often more perennial than the former. Hardy to zone 5, despite what its mild, native haunts would suggest.

One of my favorite native perennials, flowering spurge (*Euphorbia corollata*), abundant in wild areas across the eastern two-thirds of the continent, earns its creds for the space between its white flowers. And its constellations of blooms appear, fortuitously, during those few weeks in high summer when very few plants contribute anything new to the garden. It's remarkably adaptable, thriving occasionally on total neglect in my garden; I've lost it more than once in rambunctious

Euphorbia martinii 'Ascot Rainbow'.

grasses, only to watch its solitary stems defy their circumstance. It thrives on less-than-ideal soils, not surprising considering its ditchy upbringing, and deer avoid it. Tony Avent christened 'Carolina Snow' (to which he appends the common name "redneck baby's breath"—I don't think baby's breath ever were so hip); otherwise, it is painfully rare in the nursery trade. I hope someone will take notice and offer it.

In fact, many spurges give the garden a welcome dose of space. *Euphorbia martinii* 'Ascot Rainbow' is a great example, a cushion mound on a scale of twelve to fifteen inches. Terminal clusters of lime green bracts punctuated with a small red eye maintain the airy effect long after the tiny chartreuse flowers have faded. Same rules apply— deer-resistant, dry soils preferred.

NODDING

With nodding flowers and a name made from sin, it's no wonder the genus *Sinningia* is irresistible. Jon Lindstrom left American horticulture an exciting legacy, even if he was barely recognized for it in his lifetime. Besides being a professor and plant breeder at University of Arkansas, the man was a genius, seeing genera like *Sinningia* formerly relegated to high-humidity windowsills as potential rock star perennials, at least in zone 7 and above. His 'Arkansas Bells', an impressively flowered hybrid of *S. sellovii* (one of the hardiest sinningias) and *S.*

Sinningia 'Lovely'.

tubiflora, flowers as if it will never flower again, overwhelming its garden spot with desire-colored, tube skirt–shaped blooms for months.

Several of his hybrids have given rise to novelties at the hands of other breeders including the lovely 'Lovely'. Conceding its *Sinningia tubiflora* ancestry with seductively long, fragrant flowers, pink-blooming 'Lovely' forms a dense mound of fuzzy foliage, doesn't spread nearly as voraciously as its parent, and is hardy to zone 7b. Not to knock the 'rents—*S. tubiflora* is a fine plant, admired by some, cursed by others. Nobody would deny its rampant ways (it forms tubers abundantly), but oh, the scent of those flowers—some kind of warm, citrusy aphrodisiac reminiscent of a midnight tryst. What's more, hummingbirds love this stuff as much as gardeners, so you'll do good by the avian visitors to your garden, too.

Tony Avent, owner of Plant Delights Nursery, has had a hand in this hardy gesneriad business too. His 'Bananas Foster' is a smashing sinningia, topped off with hundreds of straw-shaped, banana-colored flowers for most of the growing season (now who's ready for ice cream?). It's hardy to at least zone 7b and takes summer drought like a champ, thanks to the extensive tuber system it develops underground.

Tony also gave the world another of my favorite, "hardy" gesneriads (remember, I'm a northerner struck with considerable envy)—*Seemannia nematanthodes* 'Evita'. Like any good musical theater lover, my ears perk up at the mention of lyrical references, and this groundcovering diva doesn't disappoint. Collected from 4,000 feet in Argentina, 'Evita' will also keep the hummingbirds happy as it blooms from midsummer through frost. Hardiness for so many of these is largely untested, though gardeners in zone 6 or 7 and higher should be safe to plant them out. Washington, D.C., plant breeder John Boggan is currently working with this small New World genus of African violet relatives, dreaming of their possibilities as bedding plants or container plants—a notable and worthy cause. His hybrids have color, better hardiness, and rising star power in their favor.

SASSY AND GRASSY

Grasses are about as au courant as it gets. Their recent emergence and steadfast popularity as garden staples means you have no excuse not to have five or fifty, either as specimens or in drifts. That's the beauty of grasses—with so many options, tremendous diversity, and chic appeal, they can be cast in any and all roles in your garden, from star specimen to low-key filler. And they have more to offer than the temptation of soft, curving lines waving gracefully in the wind (though that appeal alone is great)—things like fuzzy plumes, sharp spikes, and dangling pendants, for a start. In the royal theater of the plant kingdom, trees abide and grasses reign, found as they are in virtually all environments of the world, their ecological dominance an inspiration for horticulture.

Bouteloua gracilis 'Blonde Ambition'.

Tallgrass to shortgrass, carpeting mats or caespitose clumps, the world of grasses has more personalities than a garden has spaces to plant them.

It almost goes without saying that little bluestem (*Schizachyrium scoparium*), though it's native throughout the lower 48, positively dominates the native meadows and grasslands of the Great Plains. Today, there's a cultivar from almost every corner of its native distribution, with the gamut of colors and sizes represented. 'Standing Ovation', a new introduction from North Creek Nurseries, sets the standard for rigid, untoppled habit, a superb feature to capture winter's hoarfrost.

Blue grama (*Bouteloua gracilis*) is abundant on the shortgrass prairies of the High Plains, garnering its common name from its bluish leaves. Although it has a distinctly western association, blue grama is equally at home throughout the continental United States. One cultivar adapted to drought and lackluster soil, 'Blonde Ambition', is arguably one of the finest newer ornamental grasses on the market and more than a pretty face—it's a thriving choice for scree, rock, and gravel gardens, and would brighten up many urban hellstrips where turf has long given up. Clouds of blonde bristle brushes that adorn the plant from mid-August through fall inspired the cultivar's name, a floral display that lasts long after the anthers have faded and seems to only get better, right up until the winter winds blow. Discovered by High Country

Prairie junegrass (*Koeleria macrantha*).

Gardens proprietor David Salman, 'Blonde Ambition' was recognized as a 2011 Plant Select winner for something completely different on the gardening scene—a grass that thrives in the Rocky Mountains, the coasts, the Midwest, and the Southeast.

With a common name as pleasant as junegrass, you have to know that the genus *Koeleria* is full of pleasant company. On that list of grasses I couldn't garden without (and it's a mighty long list), somewhere near the top is *K. macrantha*, with a footnote that says "including all other *Koeleria*." It's native throughout most of North America, so you probably have a patch or clump growing nearby, sulking in obscurity. Known commonly as prairie junegrass, *K. macrantha* exhibits the kind of variation that drives geeks wild with excitement. It's not all for beauty, either. That it covers such a vast territory implies a generalist adaptation to climate, soils, etc., suggesting it's highly adaptable to gardens throughout the country. The form I grow in my garden is bluer than most, but even the most typical forms have remarkably clean foliage. From caespitose clumps in late spring and throughout summer, the flower heads erupt like sky-bound fireworks, lessons in the beauty of tawny and tan and reminiscent of more familiar grasses like *Calamagrostis* ×*acutiflora* 'Karl Foerster'. I simply couldn't envision a scree garden without them.

A tussocky jolt of Japanese forest grass (*Hakonechloa macra* 'All Gold').

(opposite top) European blue hair-grass (*Koeleria glauca* Coolio).

(opposite bottom) Pink muhly grass (*Muhlenbergia capillaris*).

The European blue hair-grass (*Koeleria glauca* Coolio) is another fantastic tuft for the front of border or edge of path. In my rock garden, I've encouraged its gentle reseeding, yearning for more of its miniature wheat spikes jetting from tight crowns of cool blue foliage, the coolest in the garden. On a more drastic scale, some grasses become fountains in flower, cascading grace and charm. Take pink muhly grass (*Muhlenbergia capillaris*), whose continuous clouds of color descend on the garden scene with a pinkish haze, highlighting asters and salvias with the intrigue of a smoke screen—an autumn delight.

There's something romantic about the rustle of grasses in the shade of trees—simple enough to soothe the senses and practical enough to not make a dent in the pocketbook. Consider the Japanese forest grass *Hakonechloa macra* 'Aureola', an unbeatable classic, though newer cultivars have tried to outdo its variegation ('Fubuki') or gilt ('All Gold')—unconvincingly so.

Sedges, though not true grasses, are grassy enough to be included here. In all, almost two thousand species of *Carex* populate the globe, including every continent (except Antarctica, of course). You've never met a group of plants more versatile in their horticultural applications—sun to shade, wet to dry, sedges run the gamut of ecological niches, though on balance predominate wetter situations. Their surging value as garden plants makes sense given our heightened awareness of

Carex elata 'Aurea'.

ecology. Like their grassy relatives, sedges form the vegetative bottom line in many of the ecosystems they occur in, giving style-conscious gardeners abundant templates from which to construct artful yet functional communities of plants. Books should be written about sedges as garden plants, but in the meantime, there are more than a handful with virtues worth extolling. With any luck, sedges will go down in the history of garden fashion with swagger and style.

Nestled at the edge of fifteen acres of oak-hickory timber, my childhood garden grew in the shade of stately bur oaks, whose undergrowth I took no notice of until well into my teenage years. Amid the shade garden I tried to carve out beneath those oaks, sedges (*Carex aggregata* and others) already grew. Upon conversion to the gospel of *Carex*, I planted them modestly and intentionally, fearing that as I explored the genus I might hurl headlong into yet another plant addiction. Appalachian sedge (*C. appalachica*) was one of the first, sited tenderly in the company of granite stones. As it established (easily enough) and reseeded, I only loved it more. It's a tough character, relishing dry shade and sporting long green hairs when grown lean in a variety of soils. Similarly, *C. pensylvanica*, the Pennsylvania sedge and one of our country's finest, still thrives in the dim dryness under those noble oaks. In spring, silky flowers emerge, highlighting the margins of its patchwork colonies. By midsummer it's grown to ten inches or more in height, sweeping the garden in waves of soft green. As a lawn alternative (the new age term for groundcover), it's primo.

Then there are sedges that depart from the usual soft and stolid personality. Bowles' golden sedge (*Carex elata* 'Aurea') is named for its discoverer E. A. Bowles, the great British horticulturist and writer. Grown to its fullest measure in bright light with wet feet, *C. elata* 'Aurea' is a drama queen in bold strokes of glowing chartreuse. In shade, it manages, with subdued but still vibrant colors. While its historical precedent is hard to best, modern varieties of other species fill out the roster of acid-colored sedges worth coveting. *Carex oshimensis* 'Everillo' is the latest to hit the bench from the talented Irish nurseryman Pat Fitz-Gerald. It's everything of 'Aurea' with more vigor, up to two feet across, marching to meet the morning sun in which it glows. *Carex siderosticta* 'Banana Boat' is about the best of the yellow-leaved sedges for the shady side of the water garden, maintaining strong color while not washing out completely. All sedges mentioned are reliably deer-proof.

On the complementary side of yellow, blue fescues (*Festuca glauca* and cultivars) earn all the street cred they can amass, at least in climates that, on balance, remain arid enough for them to thrive. But bring them east into gardens that receive thirty-five inches or more of water annually and you're asking for trouble—yet another cue to take note of the plants your environment has to offer you. *Carex laxiculmis* 'Hobb' (Bunny Blue) tops my list of bluish sedges that satisfy an eastern

gardener's hope for something blue and grassy—forget the false promises of blue fescue. Sure, 'Hobb' may not glow in electric blue colors emphasized by feather-fine texture (and never minding those direct mail catalogs showing otherwise, even blue fescue isn't quite *that* blue), but its ample tussocks of aquamarine blades do well enough to trigger salivation. In the shade and planted fifty at a time, it has few rivals. Though not particularly drought tolerant, it isn't picky about soil. The blue strains of *C. platyphylla*, variously called silver or satin sedge, rival those of *C. laxiculmis*, only chalkier and coarser. If there's any downside, in midwinter it does look a tad shaggy, but then again what plant still persisting in a northern temperate garden doesn't?

New on the sedge scene is 'Spark Plug', a tetraploid munchkin of *Carex phyllocephala* 'Sparkler' heritage. 'Sparkler' is hardy only to zone 7, and this dwarf offspring falls in the same category. Whether grown as a perennial or treated as an annual and dutifully tucked into containers, you can't go wrong. In a few words, it's just darn cute, with spiky swirls of foliage reaching only eight to nine inches tall. Its cream and green variegation make it an easy match to just about anything. Plus, it's deer-resistant and nearly indestructible.

Solanum pyracanthum, the infamous firethorn, is wicked in every detail, from its complementary flowers (purple) and spines (orange), to the vicious profusion of the latter. I love tucking this snarky tomato relative into containers for an element of surprise. Hardy in zones 9 through 11.

PRICKLY, POKEY, POINTY

Some plants bite back, spines and spikes out to stab any stray would-be predator (or errant gardener) who might threaten their survival. In the garden that personality warrants magnifying, especially if neighbors or the mail carrier don't rank high on your list of favorite people. From all over the world, these plants with armature make for exhilarating, if sometimes dangerous, combinations.

It's often said of cacti that they are nothing but little pricks (says the guy who still adores them). I first encountered a prickly pear cactus (*Opuntia*) as a child behind my aunt's house. In a little doorstep garden, she grew a phenomenal colony of *O. humifusa*, the eastern prickly pear cactus. She was eager to "thin them out" (an eloquent expression of distaste: she disapproved of their disheveled appearance), and I soon found myself in possession of several pads and on my way home to grow my first hardy cactus. I've been smitten from the moment its first flower unfurled, propagating it more than a dozen times since in celebration of its annual June bloom.

That was just the beginning, and in many ways my obsession with these rough and tough "roses" of the shortgrass prairies is still in its infancy. But of those I've grown and loved, *Opuntia polyacantha* tops the list of must-haves. A visit to The Flower Factory near Madison, Wisconsin, several summers ago further opened my eyes to the loveliness

Opuntia polyacantha growing at The Flower Factory, Madison, Wisconsin.

of the prickly pears and, surprisingly, their hybrids, a veritable mixology of cocktail colors soaking up their tissue petals. Reds ('Taylor's Red'), oranges ('Nebraska Orange'), and even near whites ('Crystal Tide') enchant a gardener's mind with possibilities, varying from the more usual yellow and pink forms of the species. Colorado plantsman Kelly Grummons has made it his goal to promote cold hardy cacti and sells dozens and dozens of species and varieties that challenge the notion that these plants grow only in deserts. My favorite yarn is the one where someone, staring at happy cactus clusters in the cold north, wonders how much work it must be to dig them up each fall. They're even more amazed when I grab a pair of hot dog tongs, break off a pad, toss it into a brown paper bag, and offer it to them. Yes, they're that easy.

If you're so inclined, growing cold hardy cacti like opuntias is relatively straightforward, provided a sunny exposure and sharp drainage. I'm always amazed, given their ease of cultivation, that so few people have tried them, even in hypertufa troughs. In many ways, they thrive on abuse, hailing from native environments that look better suited to archaeological digs than the cultivation of plants. These "jewels of the plains" are a centerpiece of plantsman Claude Barr's horticultural legacy (whose book of the same name has inspired more than one Midwestern plantsman, including yours truly). Barr collected dozens of cacti that persist, sad to say, mostly in collector gardens when they

Named for Claude Barr's hometown in South Dakota, *Opuntia* 'Smithwick', a purported hybrid of *O. fragilis* (to which it is often cited) and *O. cymochila*, is a flattering garden plant, despite its penchant for migrating by brittle pads across the rock garden floor.

(right) Even in their mostly spineless condition, cactus flowers are still worth swooning over. *Opuntia fragilis* var. *denudata*, denuded as it were with thumb-sized pads and morning-colored blossoms.

should enjoy wider fame. His contributions to Great Plains horticulture were innumerable, sold in pint-sized pots to fans countrywide through his ranch nursery in the southern Black Hills.

I have no idea what eryngo *means*, beyond just a vernacular permutation of the botanical *Eryngium*. But I do know eryngos are fantastic garden plants. Boasting bristly, pokey texture like nothing else can, they have that just-sharp-enough look that makes you think twice before extending your hand for a feel. Surprisingly, the genus is mostly tropical. Of course the species most grown for gardens hail from prairies and forest edges in the northern hemisphere, but if you ever consider settling in the jungle, you'll have nearly two hundred species from which to choose. Eryngos grow happily in full sun and dry soils, even dry clays—those nasty hard-packed soils that tend to bake in the summer heat. Many will reseed, but never in a way that will make you run for the hoe; in fact you should be thrilled to have more.

Smart-looking and adorably dwarf, *Eryngium planum* 'Blue Hobbit' sends up ten-inch bloom stalks from a basal rosette of blue-tinted, razor-edged leaves. Petaloid bracts subtend a conical cluster of many-ranked, stemless flowers which last for several days to a week. The staying power of all the eryngos comes from those colored bracts, which last for weeks. This one is the perfect mate for the blue-gray *Sedum telephium* ssp. *ruprechtii* 'Hab Gray' or a mat of thymes.

Old house forms of Oriental poppy.

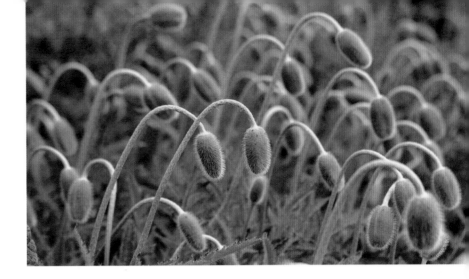

It's big, it's blue, and it's guaranteed to make a garden statement—*Eryngium planum* 'Blaukappe' tantalizes with sharp texture, persisting well after its late summer and early autumn floral spectacle with sturdy bracts. Plus that blue color isn't quick to fade, sliding into shades of gray as the growing season wanes. It carries a little more punch than 'Blue Hobbit' too, simply because of its size—a towering thirty inches tall, the perfect everlasting cut flower. If you're really brave, you could grow it in a container—think of a big galvanized barrel or blue-spackled ceramic and watch that diva steal the stage.

If you live in the mid-continent and love that prairie-style feeling, you really couldn't garden without the native rattlesnake master (*Eryngium yuccifolium*) with its eerie, almost ghostly silver flowers. No plant is truly low maintenance, but rattlesnake master comes close. It sends down a deep taproot, guaranteeing its survival and sustainability for seasons to come. You'll want to give this one a little room, since the clumps can easily grow to three feet wide in fertile soils. Like the other eryngos, it will thrive in dry to moist soils but would prefer good drainage. And if its steely silver foliage isn't enough, Tony Avent of Plant Delights Nursery introduced 'Kershaw Blue', a cultivar with striking blue-gray foliage. With so much to offer, why aren't more gardeners growing this great native?

DRUMSTICKS, CONES, AND WHIRLIGIGS

If you fancy a little whimsy in your garden, you may just need to hunt up a few balls on sticks—something like old house forms of Oriental poppy (debatedly *Papaver intermedium* or an antique form of *P. orientale*, an argument that might be more about semantics than phylogenetics). These bob with pendent, closeted buds that soon enough reveal the drama of their orange rococo dresses. Persistent in the face of neglect, these stalwart heirlooms grow in compacted soils and resent being transplanted, putting down deep taproots for a reliably annual, flamboyant reward.

(opposite top) *Eryngium planum* 'Blaukappe'.

(opposite bottom) Rattlesnake master (*Eryngium yuccifolium*).

Yellow coneflower (*Echinacea paradoxa*).

(left) *Echinacea* 'Matthew Saul' (Big Sky Harvest Moon).

A Midwestern girl goes uptown and makes it big, her name on the marquee, awash in city lights. In short, that's the story of coneflowers (*Echinacea*), whose ascendant burst onto the horticultural scene dates back to the 2003 release of 'Art's Pride' (Orange Meadowbrite) from Jim Ault's breeding program at Chicago Botanic Garden. These quintessentially summer flowers, which trace to purple coneflower (*E. purpurea*), made pretty with what they had. But from single and pink to now double and orange, this native perennial of savannas and prairies has had the ultimate makeover, even if the rouge hides a few secrets.

As nuts as I am about new coneflowers, I'll be the first to admit that there are a few lemons in the lot, and that's not just a description of their flower color. That color, though, is half the story. Meet the yellow coneflower (*Echinacea paradoxa*), an aptly named paradox. This Ozarks native takes half the credit for the litany of new colors on the market, notably for its contribution of yellow to a genus laden with pink. It's also due half the blame for the less-than-enduring nature of so many modern hybrids, which at fifteen to twenty dollars each make for some pricey annuals. For all its contributions of color, yellow coneflower is a quiet culprit. In both the garden and the wild, it is short lived, though a pleasant reseeder, taking root in the loose gravel of my scree garden with ease. On its own, it makes a fantastic garden plant, particularly when its seeds and stems dry into the autumn. Add to that its prairie

Echinacea 'Tiki Torch', here sparking a colorful conversation with nearby agastaches at Terra Nova.

(right) *Echinacea* 'Raspberry Truffle'.

cousin, the true grassland species *E. pallida* (pale purple coneflower). Its drooping, languid flowers invite crooning, even if the effect is a bit comical. Bring on the entertainment—'Hula Dancer' exaggerates the flowers' windswept swaying but is otherwise not markedly different from any other form of the species in culture or color.

Among the early hybrids, 'Matthew Saul' (Big Sky Harvest Moon) offers a robust display of green cones skirted with butternut squash rays. Many of the newer coneflowers fade to dingy versions of their formerly vibrant selves, something 'Matthew Saul' skirts by aging to pastel orange. In a sea of blue (either eryngiums or still-blooming geraniums), it's unbeatably luscious. Oranges and reds rose out of the early yellow hybrids. Varieties like 'Tiki Torch' have given rise to even newer iterations, particularly 'Flamethrower', all products of the innovative breeding at Terra Nova Nurseries. En masse, their lithe stems and tangerine daisies fill voids in modern perennial borders.

Doubles, too, are irresistible—more petals, more color. Dutch breeder Arie Blom has contributed pom-pom delicacies to the modern garden, including the delicious 'Raspberry Truffle' and the tasty 'Hot Papaya', both of which offer long stems and ample flowering time and make inventive additions to summer bouquets.

Alliums are enjoying a heyday thanks to the proliferation of bulbs used in designs by Piet Oudolf, Roy Diblik, and designers of similar

Allium schubertii.

(right) *Allium carinatum* ssp. *pulchellum* and *A. flavum*.

(opposite) Turkestan onion (*Allium karataviense*).

genre, particularly as represented by 'Summer Beauty'. They are the ultimate whirligigs, whether of the balls-on-sticks sort or exploding with many florets into a beautiful if somewhat disheveled constellation in space. Those of us who love onions lustily (at least in the ground) have around eight hundred satisfying choices, not including cultivars. Some flower in spring, others throughout the summer. Some contrast the hot colors of autumn with softer shades. It's worth planting a medley, lest you miss their geometry for a few weeks as the seasons pass from one to the next. Chief among the spring onions is one from Turkestan, *Allium karataviense*, the emergent foliage of which resembles a jade brooch. In flower, it's subtle but impactful, a pink and ivory sphere atop a short, five-inch stem which otherwise looks to roll across the garden floor. Coupled with its wide-set leaves, it is charming interplanted with sedums, sedges, and species tulips for a classy rendition on spring color. The whiter 'Ivory Queen' dominates retail sales, no less satisfactorily and with a slightly more robust constitution.

Allium schubertii, the famed volleyball onion, unleashes a zillion tiny starlets destined to terminate at the end of eerily long, unequal stalks. Against a background of grasses, they erupt from the earth in early summer to sensational effect. With no particular culture requirements, it's not surprising that more and more gardeners are planting it abundantly for drama and intrigue. And *A. carinatum* ssp. *pulchellum* and *A. flavum*

Autumn onion (*Allium stellatum*).

make devilish planting partners; in the cohort of fireworks-style onions, these starry flowers, in amethyst and yellow (respectively), shine above the rest. For a July holiday, these exploding florets spark the imagination with energy and verve.

Then there are the alliums of autumn. Species like *Allium senescens* and *A. thunbergii* give the garden spheres when most shapes have dried and shattered. *Allium senescens* joins the scene in late summer, offering lavender-pink globes in contrast to yellowing grasses. Variety *glauca* draws contrast to the lot with characteristic blue-green foliage that only softens the aesthetic—charming lavender gumdrops floating barely a foot overhead. Another cultivar, 'Blue Twister', takes the variation further, with corkscrew curly foliage adding to the same season-long flowering display. Further to the case of all-season alliums that still look good in autumn, 'Millennium', a hybrid from allium guru Mark McDonough, has made a formidable bid for best onion ever. Widely used and praised, its tough constitution and beautiful face should earn it a place in hellstrips, mixed borders, and front yard gardens across the world. If you grow only one allium, 'Millennium' might well be worth the honor.

Autumn onion (*Allium stellatum*) renews my poetic license, singing from midsummer into the waning stanza of the season while thriving in less-than-ideal soils. Its pincushion flowers sparkle into existence one

Devil's walking stick (*Aralia spinosa*) is an eastern U.S. suckering shrub with amazing durability in tough, unforgiving landscapes and a reliable display of blackberry-colored drupes that peak in late fall.

(right) *Berberis wilsoniae* and its blushing pearl berries are the poster child of the garden's sweet endings, through to their red dénouement.

rich pink floret at a time, until a stellar array at fifteen inches tall populates the garden scene. If deer threaten your sanctuary, you have little to worry about when planting autumn onions—that astringent, onion taste that even some humans find distasteful doesn't rank high on the menu for foraging megafauna, either. This Midstates native deserves greater recognition as a highly desirable garden plant in any location, but for maximum satisfaction, give it a site that encourages close inspection.

SWEET ENDINGS

Berries and drupes dangling languidly from lithe stems prove the wisdom of the old adage—save the best for last. As the garden races to a close, they are the stars of the swan song that is autumn, the sweet finale in a world of starlight romance. Dessert, anyone?

Among the sweetest fruits of a gardener's labors are the shiny beads of beautyberry (*Callicarpa*) borne in amethyst baubles. Beautyberries frequently hold the stage in gardens that know how to do fall. For two months in that season, they redeem themselves, as the rest of the garden fades into memory. Because let's face it, they verge on boring in earlier acts. The best that can be said is that they are the worthiest of irregular hedges, entertaining the gardener only with nice leaves and tiny, frothy pink flowers—until those clusters of brilliant berries appear,

The orange berries of *Triosteum perfoliatum*.

(opposite) *Callicarpa bodinieri* var. *giraldii* 'Profusion' warrants head turns from passersby in season for its profuse clusters of gorgeous berries.

multiplied in droves along the limbs of medium-sized, spreading shrubs. My first encounter with the genus was *C. dichotoma* 'Early Amethyst', a reliably zone-5-hardy cultivar that appears in plant-conscious gardens, though not as much as it should. In these cold climes, it's often grown as a dieback shrub, much like butterfly bushes. The finest fruit displays occur in conjugal communities of several plants (maximizing cross pollination is critical, of course). *Callicarpa americana* is a fabulous species for gardens warmer than zone 6; its biggest limitation in northern gardens is the lateness of its flowering season, which results in even later fruit set that tends to brush up against the first frosts. If berries are the goal, the lack of them is sort of a deal killer. But closer to its nativity—lowland areas of the boot heel of Missouri south to the Carolinas and Florida—it's an easy, turnkey shrub for foundations, hedges, or property lines that need dressing up. There are even more purple berries worth extolling—-but only one white exception worth planting. *Callicarpa japonica* 'Leucocarpa' ('Alba') puts a pallid spin on a familiar story—pearly white berries drip from descending stems; the shrub overall can reach five to six feet tall.

On a brisk late autumn walk, seed pods shake and still-hanging leaves rustle, papery sounds that signal life retreating to ground. These remnants—the leftovers from warmer days—make the winter garden bearable (if only barely for northerners) and certainly less dowdy. Leaving the seeds for winter not only pleases the eyes but birds and wildlife as well. Often still holding on late into the fall are the bizarre

The sweet ending of *Euonymus bungeanus*.

berries of *Triosteum perfoliatum*, the eastern horse-gentian. Again with the names. This zone-4-hardy herbaceous coffee relative is about as obscure as garden plants come, its predominant claims to fame tucked into the axils of four-foot-tall stems. These little oranges appear after tiny maroon flowers disappear, often without ever drawing attention to their late spring unfurling. The structure of the plant is noticeable, though—a stocky barrel-stemmed colony that looks a tad shrubby, complete with scruffy, rough-hewn leaves. Why it's not planted probably has to do with how difficult it is to propagate; it's slow from seed and recalcitrant from cuttings. If divisions are ever available, I'd advise snatching up a chunk to establish your own colony in full sun.

The mere mention of *Euonymus* can incite arguments between those repulsed by a few species' aggression and those plussed by their sordidly colored fruits. And yes, despite its red fall color, the burningbush (*E. alatus*) of fame and flagrant overplanting isn't the only euonymus worth knowing.

Few traits warrant as many words as the fruits of species like *Euonymus carnosus*, *E. atropurpureus*, and *E. bungeanus*. In almost all instances, these species grow as large shrubs, irregular in form and somewhat loose in habit. The minute and insignificant flowers, ranging from cream to white, are lost in the morass of green foliage that covers each shrub's framework through summer. Of the three mentioned, *E. carnosus* has the boldest flowering effect, though that's not saying much. Its foliage does most of the work, its leaves glossy companions to green and white flower clusters that otherwise wouldn't earn more than a dismissive, nonverbal nod. In autumn, it's a totally different story, dominated then by glossy leaves turned pink and clusters of red-capsuled fruits that last into early winter.

A similar story plays out for eastern wahoo (*Euonymus atropurpureus*), my favorite spindletree, planted by an impassioned minority as an aptly named, stick-people shrub for fencerows or the general benefit of wildlife. Its fruits in detail are dazzling—orange arils emerging from hot pink shells, profusely held by the hundreds on shrubs of indescribably variable habit—large shrub to small tree. Eastern wahoo is a geeky alternative to its blighted cousin burningbush, as it too offers excellent fall color. Finally, *E. bungeanus* sports vivid bevies of pink-turning-to-red capsules that reveal bright orange arils as winter sets in. Rounded in form and an excellent hedge or backdrop shrub, this hardy and drought-tolerant Chinese native deserves wider recognition as a choice plant for tough places.

essential
KITSCH

HORTICULTURAL ODDS AND ENDS

**The job of the artist is always
to deepen the mystery.**

—Francis Bacon, in *The Sunday Telegraph* (1964)

Some plants are essential kitsch, amounting to well-placed contradic-
tions, one-offs or oddities that exist merely because the gardener wishes
them to. They may or may not be stylish, they may not go with everything (or anything), and growing them might require a greater effort
than anything else in the ground. These are plants that you (regardless
of your preferences or tastes) grow simply because you have to—they
are like hat pins or bumper stickers or collector mugs, tchotchkes that
follow you home, that commemorate a feeling, an instinct, or some
former gardening experience. As a result, some gardens are kitschy, not
artful assemblages of thriving plants but rather collections of one truly
weird, funky thing after another. Professional horticulturists and expert
gardeners often have gardens like this; we admire them not for what
they actually grow but for the intensity of the passion required for such
a pursuit.

   In the plant world, geeky is sexy, though let's be real—not everyone
gardens for geekiness. But sometimes you need geeky, something weird
or quirky planted for conversation (even if you don't have to have all five
and join the fan club too). Beyond conversation, kitschy plants have a
way of coloring beyond the lines; they are at once slightly mysterious
and highly revealing, expressions of a garden's (and as a result a gardener's) many-layered personality. Kitschy plants are the very essence
of the best gardens, the hidden gems tucked away and treasured, the
devilishly decadent details.

In my teenage years, I had a vine fetish, which is to say I planted annual and perennial vines on anything standing upright. At some point, though, my fondness for traditional morning glories like 'Heavenly Blue' and 'Grandpa Ott's' gave way to the single-minded pursuit of one of the finest morning glories ever—the antique, choice, and consequently rare 'Sunrise Serenade', a double-flowered variety of the common *Ipomoea purpurea* with fluted fuchsia petals stacked within each other. If you have space for just one morning glory—well, I think my endorsement is clear. A common weed to some, this treasure is worth tracking down.

GARDEN ODDITIES

If I've learned anything growing up as a plant geek, it's that all my favorite gardens (and any of the best gardens I've ever been to) have at least one thing that makes you stop and go, "What the . . . ?" Yes, just like that garish lamp stand (like the one in my living room that nobody but me adores) or that cheap, ugly painting you refuse to part with, some plants will surely cause a double take—the proverbial "what the hell" is that doing here? Every garden needs at least one; something that's going to turn heads, stop traffic, and inspire conversation.

Convallaria majalis 'Vic Pawlowski's Gold'.

(right) Seashore mallow (*Kosteletzkya virginica*).

Nowadays, style-conscious people don't so much plant lily of the valley (*Convallaria majalis*) as they inherit it. The flowers have a delightful perfume, of course, but overall the plant is obnoxious and unruly, even if it colonizes dark, shady corners few other things do. There are redeeming leaves in their midst, though—a whole assortment of striped variegates like 'Vic Pawlowski's Gold' that, while a tad slow to multiply, offer a refreshing and altogether interesting alternative to the mass of green paddles otherwise associated with the genus.

On the opposite end of the horticultural spectrum in so many ways, seashore mallow (*Kosteletzkya virginica*), at nearly five feet tall in flower, ascends airily into the garden's stratosphere. A regarded native of the Southeast, this hollyhock relative of brackish swamps and backwater bayous betrays its homeland, thriving well into zone 5 and above in perfectly normal garden soils (though it wouldn't mind the wetter spots either). Relatively unknown in the garden world, it should rather be treasured for its bevies of five-petaled, cotton candy–colored, miniature-hibiscus flowers.

Michaux's bellflower (*Michauxia campanuloides*).

(left) *Cynanchum ascyrifolium*.

GHOSTS

Maybe it's a biennial. Maybe it's a short-lived perennial. It doesn't really matter. This spectral member of the bellflower family is about as kitschy, if not spooky awesome, as it comes. *Michauxia campanuloides* is anything but a generic bellflower. As it came into my view during a late summer visit to Dancing Oaks Nursery in Monmouth, Oregon, I thought I'd come across a flowering apparition in the guise of a passionflower. Eerily topping out at five feet tall, its inflorescences drip pendent white flowers that look more wraith-like than floral. All seven species of *Michauxia* are native to the Levant; the genus was named in honor of French botanist and explorer André Michaux, who had made extensive collections in the Middle East, among them this hitherto unknown bellflower, from which species his fellow botanist and countryman Charles-Louis L'Héritier de Brutelles created the genus in 1788. But I digress—how is something so creepy cool so absent from modern gardens? This native of Lebanon and Israel is hardy to zone 5 (and often underrated in hardiness), thrives in clay and rocky soils, loves full sun, freaks people out, and reseeds a little when it's all over with. How can you go wrong?

Few plants with such chic, ethereal flowers are as unsought as *Cynanchum ascyrifolium*, even as its cousin *Stephanotis* makes perennial appearances as a component of wedding bouquets and related regalia. It's versatile and adaptable—sun to part shade, poor to rich soils. Clumps thrive and persist for years, each season returning with verve and whirling stalks of flowers as they grow to an ultimate size of a few feet tall and wide.

Iris ×norrisii 'Summer Candy' is proving to be a tough, dependable bloomer in a wide range of circumstances.

LOOKS LIKE AN IRIS?

Plants manage to turn heads for many reasons. In a particular season, they might be unexpected, like the candy lilies, vesper irises, and blackberry lilies—all irises (in spite of those common names) that bloom in August, the last month anyone thinks of when they think of irises. While blackberry lilies (*Iris domestica*) have long frequented the sidewalks and fence borders of American gardens, the derivative hybrids between them and vesper irises (*I. dichotoma*) have only recently caught favor. Surely I jest, but these smashing candy lilies (as they're unfortunately known) or *I. ×norrisii* (named for Sam Norris, the originating hybridizer who I like to fancy I'm distantly related to) remind me of those ring pops that every second grader had in the '90s. They're possibly the first group of plants we'll have to market based on what time of day you're home—some bloom during the work day and others bloom at night, which explains why the geeks in the know were a little slow to get the ball rolling until now. The variation in flower color, shape, and size is quite simply vast—from the jewel-tone Dazzler series originated by Bluebird Nursery's Harlan Hamernik, including the aptly named 'Sangria', to the floriferous 'Summer Candy', one of ten or so new hybrids from Darrell Probst. In moisture-retentive soils, these candy lilies sail through droughts unscathed and in drier-than-normal soils in wet years, they'll colonize with abundance. Keep in mind that while each flower lasts for

Moraea ramosissima offers evergreen foliage and sweet-scented flowers on hip-pocket tall stems when grown in moist soils.

only one day, each plant can be laden with as many as several hundred flowers. Vigorous selections will reward you with weeks of summer color, the flowers floating in air like a diorama of paper butterflies, in the months you least expect to enjoy an iris.

Obtaining and raising stellar members of *Moraea* is worth the effort. This iris-ish genus has loads of ornamental promise, if only someone would hike the Drakensberg in South Africa, collect the hardiest forms, and distribute them to someone with a set of tweezers. In the trade, you'll find a few, mostly with cautious labels like "for collectors only." Some of these require some diligence, no doubt. But others are plenty forgiving and shouldn't suffer because someone thinks you aren't green enough in the thumbs to grow them. On trips to the West Coast, I've run into *M. huttonii* and *M. ramossisima*, both very eligible bachelorettes of the chic garden scene. Hardy in both cases to at least zone 7, with reports of *M. huttonii* persisting in reliably snowy winter climates in zone 6, these South African natives thrive in consistently moist soils, filling out into three- to four-foot plants with graceful, gladiolus-like foliage. Scapes of intricately patterned yellow flowers form in late spring and summer and, depending on the water supply, might flower steadily throughout the summer, before taking a nap. In mild winter climates these are evergreen. In the hinterlands of the northern zones, you can either pray they'll survive outside, try it, and kill a few for the

Plantago major 'Purple Perversion' takes on the best color in bright light, its shady nativity notwithstanding.

cause, or consider a container garden (which you could easily overwinter in the garage).

Yes, the theme among these species is yellow, but don't get haughty if you don't like yellow. The so-called peacock moraeas sport flowers with feathery spots that mimic beetles; biologists believe the spots entice real beetles to slip in at midnight for a naughty tryst and in the ensuing fumble, they manage to pollinate the flowers—seduction at nature's finest hour. Among these, *Moraea villosa*, *M. neopavonia*, and *M. tulbaghensis* will surely give your head a spin. As container gems, they're not difficult, though I may just be saying that to console myself (I couldn't grow them in the garden, as they aren't hardy). Drainage and a good baking summer will do the trick.

PLANTAGOS, OR THE WEEDS THAT WEREN'T

My friend, plant breeder and nurseryman Joseph Tychonievich, recently released an uber-electric version of a less-than-electric plant—plantain (*Plantago*), the leafy hosta-esque weed that you shred with the lawnmower on passes through the shadiest corners of your yard. As much as you might hate plantains, there are plenty of reasons to keep reading. The best is Joseph's 'Purple Perversion'. Tastelessly alliterative, it accurately conjures an image of a plant that dares to be purple when few others will. *Plantago major* 'Purple Perversion' came to life from a controlled cross between two varieties—'Rubrifolia' (which

Dunce's cap (*Orostachys boehmeri*).

has sort of purple foliage) and 'Frills' (which unsurprisingly has frilly leaves)—and with any luck will earn a righteous following of groupies who want to plant it and watch it reseed into a plush mat undertow, lapping at hostas in the shade ghetto. There's little point in enunciating cultural details—it's a damn purple weed. Just dig a hole (or let one reseed from the pot—they do come true from seed!).

There is at least one other reason to love plantains: 'Bowles Variety', which accessorizes its spindly, whipcord flower stalks with large, leafy bracts. Think of it as the horticultural equivalent of a crazy hat at a royal wedding. Plus, the flowers of this variety alone could have more fans on Facebook than Glenn Beck. Seriously, by now, you've got to be wondering how afflicted a plantsman has to be to name, cultivate, and produce strains of damn lawn weeds, with purple foliage no less. Genius!

QUIRKY SUCCULENTS

I would be remiss if I didn't include some succulents in this parade of oddities. Succulents are all the rage these days—they're hip, retro throwbacks to the houseplant craze, embraced outdoors for their striking textures and rugged dependability and indoors for their everlasting funk and charm.

The darling little dunce's cap (*Orostachys boehmeri*) came to my garden via a plant swap with my crazy succulent collector friend Matthew Morrow. A monocarp, this species (and others like it including *O.*

(clockwise from top left)
The flowers of hen and chicks (*Sempervivum*) add much character to ever-present rosettes.

Manfreda virginica.

Bukiniczia cabulica.

iwarenge) reseeds politely, ensuring a stable colony graces the garden scene on an annual basis with Seussical flowers, seafaring foliage, and actinomorphic rosettes. I don't think I would garden without it now. I'm sort of at a loss to elaborate on a plant so effortlessly handsome. At home in a scree garden, trough, or any location with ample drainage and sunny exposure, this petite chap, though doomed to sport his dunce-capped flowers, takes the cake for botanical entertainment.

Whole books, websites, and clubs exist in admiration of the familiar hen and chicks or houseleeks (*Sempervivum*), which many of us came to know through some cliché colony spilling out of an old boot or shoe on our grandmother's front step. We've come a long way since then. Though our grandmothers dismissed their flowers, we now appreciate these pink stars as a rare offing of a colony well established and proliferating.

I can't keep up with the names for a certain peculiar little succulent. I first encountered it as the smooth-flowing *Aeoniopsis cabulica*, since changed to *Bukiniczia cabulica*. It has no easy-to-recall common name, so I've dubbed it miniature rock cabbage (of all things, it's actually a plumbago relative). This is one of those plants so bewilderingly fabulous, you'll wonder how you've gotten along without it for this long. With speckled and splattered aquamarine foliage held in tidy rosettes, this Pakistani monocarp tops my list of essential rock garden weeds, whether grown intentionally between rocks or allowed to wander into the gravel paths around your garden. It's a reseeder when it gets around to blooming (which it does only once, usually after a couple of years of growth), sprays of pinky things that you probably won't notice at first. Leave them even if you don't admire them; its well-mannered seediness ensures a constant supply of it in the garden for many years, even after the original plants have prospered to the end of their life cycle.

When I think of weird plants, I think of *Manfreda*. Where to start—plants in this genus sort of look like agaves, with straps of succulent, rippled foliage, but they're not (though they curiously hybridize with them). Botanists get into fisticuffs over what family they belong in (don't mess with plant genealogy and expect everyone to just sleep through the revisions). The flowers have to be some of the strangest you'll ever see, looking like the frayed ends of a camel hair paintbrush.

Manfredas are dryland plants, preferring sunny conditions with drier soils and are generally best suited for gardens in zones 7 through 9. In a warm climate, they're essential kitsch. My first encounter with them came in the form of *Manfreda virginica*, a native of Ozarks glades, with eerie green flowers and often red-splattered, succulent foliage. Bewilderingly, these insignificant flowers (nobody would ever call them runway divas) emit the strangest, spicy fragrance, which emanates from five- to six-foot-tall flower stalks. Truly, truly bizarre and the only member of the genus with any real hardiness—zone 5 or 6.

In the splattered leaves department, other manfredas fill similar roles. *Manfreda longifolia* (sometimes placed in *Polianthes*) has nicely speckled foliage with toothy edges, and the flowers of this native of Texas and Mexico are some of the prettiest of the agave clan—pinkish stars that burn out to red. And oh, the smell! Several intergeneric hybrids exist between *Manfreda* and *Polianthes*, most of which are collector novelties and not widely available. The results? Larger flowers in colors ranging from pink to near black, that cloying fragrance, and even hardiness to zone 6b. If these hybrids get into commercial production, they'll be perfect for a dry garden near the back door, where you can appreciate the details while growing the plants in superb drainage.

One of the more popular of these bizarre agave-ish plants, *Manfreda undulata* 'Chocolate Chips' boasts pronounced chocolate-splattered, rippled leaves that even casual gardeners recognize as something special. A Carl Schoenfeld plant from Yucca Do Nursery, 'Chocolate Chips' has surprising hardiness despite its Mexican origins, with some reports of thriving, flowering plants as far north as zone 6b. In midsummer on established plants, NASA-inspired flowers blast into orbit atop a three-foot solitary stalk.

Griffinia liboniana, potted, flowering from the shady steps of Robyn Brown's Nashville garden.

CONTAINING YOURSELF

The kitschiest gardens always have containers, maybe because the kitschiest gardeners always need one more space to tuck in a few of their collected treasures. Whether you garden on an expansive lot or on a balcony, containers are invaluable in the modern garden—in one instance for relief of scale, in another for the relief of having a place to plant the latest round of impulse buys. While theoretically anything can be grown in a container (even if not for very long or very well), in practice, there are just some plants that look classiest when spilling from ceramics, faux bois, or some repurposed object screaming for a second life in horticultural theater. Container gardens can preview other elements of your garden—dramatic textures, exotic specimens, and the like—but they certainly don't have to be anything more than a vessel for well-planted odds and ends.

I fell in love with *Griffinia liboniana* the first time I saw it—a Brazilian bulb with succulent, plastic leaves and feathery blue flowers held on slender ascendant stems that couldn't have looked better even if it wasn't in an unassuming terra cotta pot. In the northern hemisphere, this regular of the tropical understory will thrive only in a container, set out on the patio for the summer and brought into the heat of the house in winter. The seeming effortlessness of one container

(opposite top) *Eucomis vandermerwei* 'Octopus' growing in a terra cotta container on the front steps of garden designer Troy Marden's Nashville home.

(opposite bottom) In this trough growing on my friend Mike Kintgen's front doorstep in Denver, two plants clamored for my attention—first, the soothing blue flowers of *Eritrichium* and second, the comical claws of *Lamium garganicum*, a tiny cousin of the familiar spotted deadnettle (*L. maculatum*) that's probably pillaging your shady backyard while you read this.

of *G. liboniana* on your outdoor dining set will surely convince your friends that Martha has nothing on you. Move it around the garden for photoshoot-quality styling from almost any angle.

Then of course there are the pineapple lilies (*Eucomis*), which seem to be closing in on the apex of the botanical clock—hitting the stride of their popularity for their tropical textures and loudmouth performances in the heat of summer. In general, they come in three versions: big, small, and weird. Among the big, *E. pole-evansii* takes the cake for her colossal, stately columns of green—green leaves, green stalks, green flowers, green fruits—measuring in at just under five feet tall. There are plenty of smaller eucomis if you're feeling pinched for space but still want a generous dose of South African charm. The leaves of 'Glow Sticks' from Terra Nova Nurseries are gently ruffled; they emerge apricot and age to something resembling peach bisque. 'Sparkling Burgundy' is another talked-about favorite, growing only twenty inches tall but sparkling in, well, burgundy, merlot, and a range of purples, depending on the time of day. In containers, it's one of my favorites, even if it never stalks up its starry pink flowers.

And then the weird. 'Dark Star', a seeming Star Wars set prop and sea urchin hybrid, is either downright cool or creepy, depending on your personality. Spikes of pink flowers appear in midsummer, which tone down the weird, a little (or enhance the punk?). 'Octopus', a selection of the naturally dwarf *Eucomis vandermerwei*, could be the weirdest of the bunch if polling tracked such trends. Barely six inches tall and up to a foot wide, about the only place to appreciate something quite so diminutive and obscure is in a container. Had I known of the existence of this plant as a child, I would never have needed a pet. The flowers up the ante on cuteness and with its vigor, you'll have a living bouquet of them in one season.

If tropicals don't inspire you or fit your niche, why not carve out a rock (or fashion something similar with hypertufa) and plant some alpines? Hypertufa troughs—molded amalgamations of Portland cement, peat moss, and perlite—make perfect homes for a whole palette of plants that would challenge many of us to grow in the open garden.

On an herbal note, scented geraniums, long the pampered prizes of herb collectors, are poised for a renaissance. After all, these aren't your typical front-porch red geraniums. Scented geraniums have obviously tactile qualities—flagrant stroking, touching, and caressing is encouraged, if only to indulge in the phenolic phenomena exuded from their variously shaped leaves. The names they trade under seem more descriptive than qualified cultivar names or replace the latter altogether. My present fascination with them is two-fold—they are a horticultural constant, the perfect plant to engage with during summer and winter months (whatever the temperatures of the beverage, scented geraniums are natural companions). In summer they reside

The devilishly dark flowers of *Pelargonium sidoides*.

(opposite) *Pelargonium crispum* 'Cy's Sunburst'.

on the deck, patio, or balcony ledge. In winter, they call the windowsill home. Consider *Pelargonium crispum* 'Cy's Sunburst', a variegated form of the familiar fingerbowl lemon-scented geranium. With fascinatingly curly leaves, adpressed to one another along rigid, ascendant stalks, 'Cy's Sunburst' cries out for inspection via fingertips. Discovered by Cyrus Hyde of Well-Sweep Herb Farm in Port Murray, New Jersey, this relatively new cultivar demands greater use as container specimen, collected if also coddled, even though it's a cinch to grow.

I was first struck by *Pelargonium sidoides* on a trip to California, its long-stemmed aerial flowers cast down over the path, inviting scrutiny and admiration. In a patio container in my own garden a few years later, I staged it against a textural background of midsummer green for unhindered, up-close-and-personal staring. Even when not in flower, which is a rare few weeks a year if given enough water and light, its minted foliage maintains a crisp silver ruffle and spicy fragrance when crushed.

Dodecatheon 'Amethyst', a shooting star hybrid of interspecific origins.

(below) *Cyclamen coum* 'Something Magic'.

LEAN IN

A thousand or so garden plants have flowers so small, you'll have to slow down and lean in for a closer look. People in a hurry call these a waste of time, and they'll probably keel over from a heart attack in a hedge of barberries outside their office building—a sad fate. Small plants cause us to savor the garden, beckoning us to kneel or peer in appreciation. A garden shouldn't scream all the time but instead embrace the contrast between big and small, coarse and fine. Little flowers and tiny leaves belong in the intimate nooks and crannies of the garden—alongside paths, for example—or in any accessible spot, so you can appreciate their fineries as up close and personal as you like. But no matter the details, they should be worth the effort, packing a punch despite their size, whether visually, texturally, or olfactorily.

Take, for instance, shooting stars (*Dodecatheon*). The shooting stars of mountain streamside fame deserve recognition for their spring flowers, which—like their common name—last only a moment. In droves, they are essential details; as singles, they'd be lost in the robust bustle of any normal spring garden. Or consider cyclamen, which collectors coo for, prized for their pewter and jade patterned leaves. Depending on the species, these come complete with little flowers in either spring or fall. *Cyclamen coum* 'Something Magic', a zone-4-hardy selection, may carpet the garden with pink flowers in late winter, but its foliage rivals the falling leaves for interest and color. Many nurseries have good strains of *C. coum* and *C. hederifolium* for sale.

FRITILLARIES

Several years ago as an intern at *Better Homes & Gardens* tasked with de-accessioning the garden department's library, I stumbled upon a monograph about fritillaries and proceeded to jump head first into a genus that I knew practically nothing about. In the end I killed most that I acquired that summer, one of many horticultural lessons from the school of hard knocks. In my overzealousness to get my hands on as many as I could find, I overplanted the garden with them, many in conditions that weren't much to their liking. Don't mistake me—most are not difficult to grow; they just require someone with half a brain and five minutes of forethought to plant them. Here's five minutes and two cents' worth about the species that survived my initial torture and that I've since come to adore.

Fritillaries offer a little something for everyone. If you're a rock gardener and want to grow the rarest, strangest thing you can get your hands on, there are plenty of species to try your luck with (that's an afterhours conversation we can save for later, but to get a head start, Google *Fritillaria striata* and *F. sewerzowii* and put on some mood

Fritillaria pallidiflora.

(opposite) Lebanese fritillary (*Fritillaria elwesii*).

music). If you want some dangling bells of weird awesomeness without too much hassle, a few species offer a solid beginning.

Fritillaria meleagris is probably the most available fritillary apart from the giant imperial fritillary (*F. imperialis*), showing up in small bins and dimly lit corners of the garden center or big box store. Don't be scared: even if it looks like a snake's head, it doesn't bite—too hard. Dangly and egg-sized, these flowers come in white, green, and burgundy, often with substantial checkering or tessellation (use that one in a crossword, Will Shortz!). They're so shamefully simple to grow, it's a wonder we don't see them in gardens more often. Another great bulb for the shade garden.

Lebanese fritillary (*Fritillaria elwesii*) is a good case study for the magnitude of "matter" found within the fritillaries. Grape-shaped green flowers often sport exterior black markings that sweep out to flaring edges, with occasional hints of gold in the throat that make me weak in the knees. Plant a few clumps of these between your daffodils, and your neighbors will really think you've got some attitude. It's a vigorous grower, but rarely weedy, and doesn't mind a little shade; after all, we wouldn't want your emerging hosta spears to be lonely.

One of the most perennial fritillaries I've cultivated is *Fritillaria pallidiflora*. These chartreuse to primrose-colored flowers make happy companions to almost any spring-flowering perennial or bulb, meaning you can plop them in with effortless precision and show up the Joneses and Martha in the process. Toss in a few hellebores and some Virginia bluebells (*Mertensia*) for good measure, and you've made art. Each candelabra-like stem boasts three to five or more flowers that age to pink-blushed shades of parchment. Pretty as they are, don't smell them and thank me later, unless you have a penchant for acrid odors. In the woodland garden, they're a surefire hit, thriving in humusy soils amid liberally planted colonies of *Dicentra eximia* or *Corydalis*. They'll certainly tolerate worse, but you'll sacrifice a few flowers in the process. But even after tradeoffs for soil, what a spectacular plant to jazz up any number of April-barren spots in your garden.

Bishop's cap (*Mitella diphylla*).

THE BASTARD SAXIFRAGES

Mitella and *Tellima*, the anagrammed saxifragaceous cousins of coral bells, have languished backstage while *Heuchera* has gone on parade. While these genera don't pack the punch of the coral bells' wildly marked leaves, their flowers are worth a look, especially if you're looking for something a little more subdued.

    Mitella will probably never get any respect in a fast-paced world, appreciated instead by those with heads firmly affixed in the botanical clouds. But tiny or not, these flowers are damn cool. Hanging from rocky cliffs in woodlands across the eastern United States, these ephemerals announce the arrival of spring each year with bottlebrushes of little white flakes that have charmed me since my early college days. Escaping to a local state park in early April each year to avoid real studying, I instead studied the subtleties of *M. diphylla* foliage, occasionally encountering forms flushed with a bit of bronze, conjuring thoughts of what it must have been like for early plant breeders to delve into the colors lurking in coral bell leaves. Since those discoveries on rainy afternoons, I have embraced these native groundcovers as chic filler in my shade garden, planting them in abundance at the margins of hostas, epimediums, and hellebores, the supporting cast to showier stars. They don't last long, but who cares. It's one more excuse to plant something else to take their place.

Fringecups (*Tellima grandiflora*).

Ranked by magnitude of flower power, *Tellima grandiflora* bests many coral bells, flurrying the late spring garden with columns of suspended white snowflakes that age to pink. Up close, the flowers have noticeably frilly edges and are worth a minute or two of close investigation.

LITTLE HARDY ORCHIDS

The word "orchid" scares the hell out of some people. This amazing family of plants so often has the undeserved reputation of being hard to grow, fussy, and exclusively tropical. Fear not—a cadre of hardy terrestrial orchids awaits horticultural celebration. But don't confuse these orchids' raffish appearance with the trumped-up, tropical flowers of supermarket fame—these aren't orchids by generic definition.

Goodyera pubescens (rattlesnake plantain) is a great place to start. It's mostly grown for its startling ivory-veined leaves and not for its small, white, fly-pollinated flowers, but who's keeping track? Forming a groundcover in a few years, this native orchid of the Southeast loves shade and a moist humusy soil. *Aplectrum hyemale* (puttyroot orchid) enjoys similar conditions and shares a range with the latter. Brownish flowers with hints of green and violet stippling populate the ends of foot-high flower stalks. Both are best appreciated en masse; leave them to colonize and form arrays.

Spiranthes cernua 'Chadd's Ford'.

Nicer still are the lady's tresses, the late summer- and autumn-blooming members of the genus *Spiranthes*, known for their fragrance and spiraled stalks of ivory flowers. Small and white or not, the fragrance of these surprise-you-when-you're-least-expecting-it orchids is enough to plant them out in droves. By September when it rolls around to flowering, I've long forgotten *S. cernua* 'Chadd's Ford' from the year before. But like spears of asparagus, the flower stalks push up through the leaves and ajuga mat, offering a brief floral display akin to a quick bite of dessert after a satiating meal. In autumn, new flowers are simply the best, particularly when they smell this sweetly good. I've abused mine in the garden for years, planting them near rocks in dry shade, in the shade of monkshoods (*Aconitum*) and yellow waxy bells (*Kirengeshoma*) and tickled underfoot by sedges hell-bent on colonizing the backyard. They haven't missed a fall yet.

WEEDY AND RESEEDY

In my own gardens, I've always tried to foster serendipity when possible. Serendipity with a horticultural bent is the unintended consequence of growing living things, because let's face it: plants—whether cultivated in the garden or free-flowering in the wild—have evolved means to migrate. I've always tended to appreciate reseeding; it makes me think plants are situated enough to spread themselves, albeit occasionally with unwelcome vengeance. Sometimes, the best ideas just crop up in the garden, right? Certainly in the wild, if a plant flowers and sets seed, those seeds have at least a passing chance of germinating and beginning a new generation. But the garden, just like the wild, is an environment with its own mechanics. What might reseed with vengeance in your garden might very well languish in solitariness in mine. Regardless, in some circumstances some plants will invariably become weedy. It's up to you to decide if that's such a bad thing or not. If you see reseeding as a nuisance, you might scan this section as a recommended list of plants to avoid—like any repentant soul, you know it's easier to just avoid temptation than to correct sin. If you perceive reseeding as a gift, these odds and ends are a shopping list. As Ralph Waldo Emerson cheerily professed, a weed is "a plant whose virtues have not yet been discovered."

PURPLE AND PLUSH

Violets charmed more than a few of us as kids, springing up in turf in purple posies, the angst of anyone striving for the monocultured, manicured lawn. Those little pips were the weedy *Viola sororia*, the common blue violet that some of us picked and presented with pride to our mothers on her honored day. But we're big kids now, and as grown-ups, there are a whole lot of classy violets that our gardens shouldn't be without. And unsurprisingly, they're a cinch to grow.

If you want a little plant that packs some punch, spruce up the shade with *Viola walteri* 'Silver Gem'. Discovered at Mt. Cuba Center in Delaware, this native Appalachian violet may share space with your feet but deserves all the attention of something staring you in the face. Why? Frosted silver foliage, which never seems to look bad, even in droughts, is why. The flowers are the usual fare—little purple things from early spring through fall, reblooming sporadically until frost.

With your hosta ghetto successfully gentrified, you can't forget that sun-baked pile of rocks in the front yard that you call a rock garden. You have three violet options here—*Viola pedata* (bird's foot violet), *V. egglestonii* (glade violet), and *V. corsica* (Corsican violet). These three species are more likely to die from your kindness than from neglect. In the case of the first two, they occur natively on limestone crests, suffering through miserably high pH soils in the company of sedges and rattlesnakes. Seriously, give them a rocky fissure, some pebbles, and a little water to get established and you're on your way. Once established you can hope they'll reseed. The flowers of *V. pedata* are more than worth a little trouble, ranging in color patterns from zippy bicolors to bold selfs. *Viola egglestonii* forms mounds of attractive, dissected foliage with traditional purple flowers usually less variable than *V. pedata*. *Viola corsica* comes as close as any on this list to epitomizing a pansy in perennial form. Its sheer floriferousness is mind-blowing—in many climates you can expect at least six months of semi-continuous flowering, with generous shows in the spring and fall when nights are cool. Unlike the other two rock garden options, it appreciates a tad more water and a bit richer soil—cheap prerequisites for an A-list plant.

If pandas and teddy bears make you all warm and fuzzy, why not plant a garden with fuzzy bells worth petting? If ever you were told not to touch plants in the garden, ignore that advice and take mine: it's absolutely okay to play with your plants. They won't mind. In fact one of the singular reasons to grow pasqueflowers (*Pulsatilla*) is for the tactile satisfaction of their silky flowers and puffy seedheads. The genus *Pulsatilla* is a classic among rock gardeners and also a favorite of botanists for taxonomic target practice: its forty-some species, which offer tussocks of anemone-like flowers cloaked in a super-soft pubescence rivaling the plushest wool, are sometimes lumped in with *Anemone*. Double, semi-double, red, purple, gray, yellow, and white hardly begin to describe the menu available. *Pulsatilla patens* (prairie crocus) is one of my favorites and the harbinger of spring in shortgrass prairies and meadows across the midsection of the continent. It's incredibly cold hardy, often weathering through late freezes and cold snaps without damage. In the garden any of the pulsatillas, including the more common *P. vulgaris*, are just as happy in average soils at the edge of borders or beds as they are between stones, making company with nearby daffodils or crocuses on their spring-bound voyage. Keep

Corsican violet (*Viola corsica*).

Pulsatilla patens, one of dozens of beautiful pasqueflowers worth pursuing.

drainage in mind though—you don't want soaked or (worse yet) rotten pasqueflowers. Hardiness runs in the family, and pasqueflowers often weather through late freezes and cold snaps without injury. If you're in search of something funky, seek out the lemon lime *P. aurea* or the plush burgundy *P. rubra* ssp. *hispanica*.

A FEW ANNUALS FOR GOOD MEASURE

The first plant I recall reseeding like it owned the place was probably money plant (*Lunaria annua*), an old-fashioned biennial that seems to have fallen out of favor over time. I can't understand why—to this day, nearly everyone who visits my garden asks for a few "coins" to start their own patch. It reseeded like Genghis Khan conquered Asia— ruthlessly and with vindictive determination. But I didn't mind. In spring, the purple or white cruciform flowers brightened up the cottage garden, and even in years when the rest of the garden didn't seem to come along like I'd hoped, those happily virulent biennials held on. As biennials—plants that live a two-part life cycle, spending the first year in leaf and the second and final year in flower—their ferocity was easily forecasted by the degree to which they carpeted the ground the year before flowering, and if I didn't approve of their numbers, they pulled easily. As a plant known better to 19th-century gardening journals than 21st-century gardeners, it's had more than a few notable cultivars over

California poppies (*Eschscholzia californica*) come in a wild assortment of colors, readily available from finer seed dealers who've made the effort to sort them into strains. Nothing beats these blaring orange petals arising from marine green foliage.

the years. The distinctive 'Rosemary Verey', named for its discoverer, the venerable British garden designer, is about as punk as the lot gets— lacquered purple foliage with specks of green sassily complement neon violet flowers. If there is such a thing as "traditional" variegation, you can find varieties of money plant with white-splashed green foliage and white flowers, usually with a name like 'Variegata Alba' or something similar (multiple names happen, okay?). On a scale of edginess, the look is brazen, but not ballsy. 'Pennies in Bronze' offers the show its name implies. Purse-worthy pennies replace tan, translucent coins at maturity, aging from green to shades of copper and bronze that scintillate in the evening sun. Nothing rivals the effect.

At some point in college I fell in love with simple, carefree California poppies (*Eschscholzia californica*). I hauled out half a dozen packets and gleefully cast the seeds about my new scree garden. The colors ranged from buttery cream to wild rose and of course the usual bright yellows and oranges. Grown from various mixes I'd picked up at some end-of-season sale and stashed for another year, these emblematic poppies bloomed from mid-May through the first hard freeze. Native throughout the western United States, these poppies have graced gardens for nearly two centuries. By any measure, they're harmless weeds, technically perennials but behaving like annuals, keen to reseed and reinstate themselves with verve even where they shouldn't grow. If you don't like

Nicotiana mutabilis.

(opposite) *Nicotiana glutinosa.*

where they land, they pull out with remarkable ease. There's otherwise not much to say about a plant so familiar and well known, except that annual reinstallations keep your populations thriving with jolts of new color—harbingers of season-long happiness.

It seems that flowering tobaccos (*Nicotiana*) are on the cusp of a modern renaissance and thankfully so, given the catalog of choices available to gardeners. At one point in horticultural history, gardeners could count on encountering *N. alata* each spring, in its various color forms in packs at the garden center. These carefree flowerers have given way to more select forms and species of antique provenance. Passed along and preserved in heirloom circles, many of these species and cultivars enjoyed acclaim in yesteryears only to slip from fad to forgotten—cue a list of *N. sylvestris*, *N. langsdorfii*, and even *N. rustica*, which fine garden plants are popularly available from many heirloom seed producers. The former, beloved for its curvaceous, drooping white flowers, is starkly different from the other two, which have smaller, pendent flowers in green and yellow, respectively. But in the spirit of antique flowers, *N. glutinosa* offers some of the loveliest, even if it takes some imagination to believe it's actually a flowering tobacco. Its flower, while pendent, more closely resembles a campanula blushed in rosy peachy tints. Like the rest, though, it's weedily painless to grow, perfect to fill space and time in a variety of garden niches. A newer species recently described from Brazil, *N. mutabilis*, has been championed by leading garden designers thrilled with its towering, four- to five-foot-tall architecture and abundant flowers, blushed pink at first and then aging to white.

CONCLUSION

LAST CALL

A late summer silhouette in my garden.

Horticulture is about people, plants, and passion, and in that order. It's an act of humanity borne from passionate interaction with plants. In the course of this book, I hope I've connected those dots to a more fertile result.

No matter how you cut it, gardening is contrived. No matter the ingredients, no matter the context, the result is always art, a fruitful, beautiful place for living in general and reveling in fine plants specifically. It may evoke nature, even attempt to recreate it, but it's still a human enterprise, which makes it all the more important to choose to live with the earth, not against it. No gardener has ever set out to harm the earth, but we do sometimes find too many reasons to do battle against it.

With any luck this book doesn't end here. I wish for it to be a beginning—a Google search for something you didn't know, even a trip to the bookshelf to thumb through a masterwork you haven't read yet. Maybe you'll take a trip to the garden center, poking around and perusing the shelves in search of the next kitschy plant. Perhaps you'll give mail-order gardening a try if you don't nab your quarry. Maybe you'll carve out an entirely new garden, hell-bent on giving yourself license to plant passionately. Don't become hindered by the so-called rules, either. Rules are meant to be broken. They give us order, though often little guidance to be better gardeners. Break them habitually, and learn from the results. Any insights offered here grew from the ground, flowered in my head, and set seed as words on these pages. The next season is up to you. I hope some seedlings of advice will sprout and grow.

The categories presented in this book were not intended to be absolute or all-encompassing, but rather playful and perhaps inspired groupings for conversing about an ever-inspiring gallery of plants worth planting. Remember, plants don't read the same books we do. They are organisms, surviving and thriving as a product of their genetics, influenced by the environment in which they grow. Often, they'll surprise you. Don't let on. They don't need to hear they aren't supposed to be doing that thing they aren't supposed to be doing.

At the end of the day, you just have to get out there and plant. You have to plant what you know and reap the lessons of what you don't. You have to commit to the earth, one growing season at a time. Failure is not only inevitable, it's encouraged. Screw something up. Kill a plant or five. You don't even have to learn botanical Latin to be a successful gardener, but if your ear starts to pick it up, you can't go wrong. For many of us, it's a language learned as some do Spanish or French in high school, just as practical and as lovely to hear. As the sun sets each day, the only rules that apply to the modern eclectic garden are to cultivate thriving plants and to let passion for the pursuit reign.

ACKNOWLEDGMENTS

Inevitably, this nod to the Patient Many is the last thing an author writes before submitting a manuscript, and this is intentional. It's a risky business—the fear of making lists of people causes even veteran writers to quake. None of us lives in a bubble, even if we retire to them occasionally. The balance of our work is influenced by countless people, and this list is a snapshot of those who've made this book, and the passion documented herein, possible.

Tom Fischer—the single most patient editor I've ever known. Thank you, really.

Benjamin Futa—whose phone call back in September 2011 was the tipping point for a wave of important thoughts that coalesced in this book. Words cannot thank you enough for calling that day, dear friend!

Dan Heims—my sensei and close friend, whose vision and taste for "wow" plants will always inspire me. As the original, self-proclaimed hortiholic, he's had a great influence on my career, and thus, residually, on this book.

Elvin McDonald and Ken Druse—wise counselors, whose garden writing always seems to be the right thing I need to hear at the right time.

Joseph Tychonievich—my gardening best friend and a tour de force in his own right, for his input, critiques, and general good humor when it comes to listening to me ramble for hours about sundry subjects.

Lindsey Smith-McCartney—my best friend and "family" editor, who often answers phone calls from me that begin with "I need an adjective . . ."

In addition to the aforementioned, all the modern plantsmen and plantswomen that I look up to in pursuit of plants, whose work motivates me to carry on in this tradition of bringing great plants to the attention of passionate gardeners—Panayoti Kelaidis, Dan Hinkley, Tony Avent, Jim Ault, Stephanie Cohen, Steve and Caroline Bertrand, Roy Diblik, Allen Bush, and so many others noted throughout the text. As another generation of young horticulturists rises in their work, it's my hope that the knowledge and advancements of the last fifty years carries forward with verve and energy in pursuit of even more great plants for great gardens.

To all my friends, colleagues, and family who at some point listened to me kvetch about this project over the course of its long genesis. I'm sure it got old.

Finally, to the team of passionate people that I have the pleasure of working with every day at the Greater Des Moines Botanical Garden, led by luminary President and CEO Stephanie Jutila. If I weren't surrounded by such talented and dedicated people, I would surely be less in my profession. A special shout-out to "Botany's New Boys," as the New York Times described them—Winston Beck, Tyler Johnson, and Josh Schultes—along with Leslie Hunter and Nenad Tatalovic.

USEFUL CONVERSIONS AND HARDINESS ZONES

INCHES	CENTIMETERS
1/4	0.6
1/2	1.25
3/4	1.9
1	2.5
1 1/4	3.1
1 1/2	3.8
1 3/4	4.4
2	5.0
3	7.5
4	10
5	12.5
6	15
7	18
8	20
9	23
10	25
12	30
15	38
18	45
20	50
24	60
30	75
32	80
36	90

FEET	METERS
1	0.3
1 1/2	0.5
2	0.6
2 1/2	0.8
3	0.9
4	1.2
5	1.5
6	1.8
7	2.1
8	2.4
9	2.7
10	3.0
12	3.6
15	4.5
18	5.4
20	6.0

AVERAGE ANNUAL MINIMUM TEMPERATURE

ZONE	TEMPERATURE (°F)	TEMPERATURE (°C)
1	below -50	below -46
2	-50 to -40	-46 to -40
3	-40 to -30	-40 to -34
4	-30 to -20	-34 to -29
5	-20 to -10	-29 to -23
6	-10 to 0	-23 to -18
7	0 to 10	-18 to -12
8	10 to 20	-12 to -7
9	20 to 30	-7 to -1
10	30 to 40	-1 to 4
11	40 to 50	4 to 10

For more details and to see the USDA Hardiness Zone Map, visit planthardiness.ars.usda.gov.

TEMPERATURES

$$°C = 0.55 \times (°F - 32)$$

$$°F = (1.8 \times °C) + 32$$

INDEX